# TOXIC CHARITY

# TOXIC CHARITY

*How Churches and Charities Hurt Those They Help (And How to Reverse It)*

## ROBERT D. LUPTON

HarperOne
*An Imprint of HarperCollinsPublishers*

HarperOne

HarperCollins books may be purchased for educational, business, or sales promotional use. For information please write: Special Markets Department, HarperCollins Publishers, 10 East 53rd Street, New York, NY 10022.

HarperCollins website: http://www.harpercollins.com

HarperCollins®, 📖®, and HarperOne™ are trademarks of HarperCollins Publishers.

FIRST EDITION

Library of Congress Cataloging-in-Publication Data is available upon request.

ISBN 978–0–06–207620–5

11 12 13 14 15   RRD(H)   10 9 8 7 6 5 4 3 2 1

# Contents

# TOXIC CHARITY

# Chapter One

## *The Scandal*

In the United States, there's a growing scandal that we both refuse to see and actively perpetuate. What Americans avoid facing is that while we are very generous in charitable giving, much of that money is either wasted or actually harms the people it is targeted to help.

I don't say this casually or cavalierly. I have spent over four decades working in inner-city Atlanta and beyond, trying to develop models of urban renewal that are effective and truly serve the poor. There is nothing that brings me more joy than seeing people transitioned out of poverty, or neighborhoods change from being described as "dangerous" and "blighted" to being called "thriving" and even "successful." I have worked with churches, government agencies, entrepreneurs, and armies of volunteers and know from firsthand experience the many ways "good intentions" can translate into ineffective care or even harm.

Almost 90 percent of American adults are involved personally or financially in the charity industry. Our entire society—from school children to corporate CEOs, from small churches to massive government agencies—upholds the wonderful value that helping others is a big part of the American character. "Today there's a 'compassion boom' of people helping others," says Patrick Corvington, CEO of the federal Corporation for National and Community Service. Unlike during difficult economic times in the past when volunteerism declined, charitable service today continues to increase. A recent poll by the Orlando *Parade* (March 7, 2010) confirms that more than 90 percent of Americans believe that it is "important to be personally involved in supporting a cause we believe in" in their communities and in the world at large. And Americans are working hard to hand down this value to the next generation.

Public service has moved beyond mere catchphrase or school requirement in our country. It is now a way of life for Americans of all ages. Nearly every church, business, and organization gets involved in some sort of service project. College spring-break service projects and church mission trips have become the norm. Corporations realize they can enhance their images through cause-related marketing while also building up employee loyalty and pride in the company. The compassion industry is almost universally accepted as a virtuous and constructive enterprise.

But what is so surprising is that its outcomes are almost entirely unexamined. The food we ship to Haiti, the well we dig in Sudan, the clothes we distribute in inner-city Detroit—all seem like such worthy efforts. Yet those closest to the ground—on the receiving end of this outpouring of generosity—quietly admit that it may be hurting more than helping. How? Dependency. Destroying personal initiative. When we do for those in need what they have the capacity to do for themselves, we disempower them.

Africa can serve as a large-scale example of the problem. In the last fifty years, the continent has received $1 trillion in benevolent aid. How effective has this aid been? Country by country, Africans are far worse off today than they were a half century ago. Overall per-capita income is lower today than in the 1970s. Over half of Africa's 700 million population lives on less than $1 a day. Life expectancy has stagnated, and adult literacy has plummeted below pre-1980 levels. "It's a kind of curse," says Dambisa Moyo, an African economist and the author of *Dead Aid*. Aid, though intended to promote health, becomes "the disease of which it pretends to be the cure."

A similar devastation has been inflicted upon the subsidized poor of our own country (though admittedly not as extreme). For all our efforts to eliminate poverty—our entitlements, our programs, our charities—we have succeeded only in creating a permanent underclass, dismantling their family structures, and eroding their ethic of work. And our poor continue to become poorer.

In over forty years working with the urban poor in inner-city Atlanta and around the globe, I have learned that it takes more than high ideals to bring about substantive change in populations of need. The organization I founded, Focused Community Strategies, has worked diligently to sort out, by trial and error, which efforts result in actual transformation and which efforts have results that are ultimately noxious and harmful.

Still, I continually witness profoundly broken systems in nonprofit work. Many people legitimately fault the government for decades of failed social programs, and yet frequently we embrace similar forms of disempowering charity through our kindhearted giving. And religiously motivated charity is often the most irresponsible. Our free food and clothing distribution encourages ever-growing handout lines, diminishing the dignity of the poor while increasing their dependency. We converge on inner-city neighborhoods to plant flowers and pick up trash, bruising the pride of residents who have the capacity (and responsibility) to beautify their own environments. We fly off on mission trips to poverty-stricken villages, hearts full of pity and suitcases bulging with giveaway goods, trips that one Nicaraguan leader describes as effective only in "turning my people into beggars."

Giving to those in need what they could be gaining from their own initiative may well be the kindest way to destroy people.

We mean well, our motives are good, but we have neglected

to conduct care-full due diligence to determine emotional, economic, and cultural outcomes on the receiving end of our charity. Why do we miss this crucial aspect in evaluating our charitable work? Because, as compassionate people, we have been evaluating our charity by the rewards we receive through service, rather than the benefits received by the served. We have failed to adequately calculate the effects of our service on the lives of those reduced to objects of our pity and patronage.

What have we missed? As reported by Dambisa Moyo in *Dead Aid*, a World Bank study found that 85 percent of the aid money flowing into African countries never reaches the targeted areas of need and often goes to unproductive (if not blatantly corrupt) uses.

Expenditures for a week of service by church and college groups are grossly out of proportion with what is actually accomplished. U.S. mission teams who rushed to Honduras to help rebuild homes destroyed by hurricane Mitch spent on average $30,000 per home—homes locals could have built for $3,000 each. The money spent by one campus ministry to cover the costs of their Central American mission trip to repaint an orphanage would have been sufficient to hire two local painters and two new full-time teachers and purchase new uniforms for every student in the school.

Each year religious mission trips consume billions of dollars (estimates run from $2.5 to $5 billion annually), junkets that put some tourist dollars into local economies but seldom yield appreciable improvement in the lives of those being served. What appears to be extravagant, selfless, even sacrificial investments from caring benefactors may well be exposed as large-scale misappropriations of charitable resources.

To be sure, not all charitable response is toxic. The immediate outpouring of aid in times of catastrophe is inspiring and lifesaving. When an earthquake and tsunami devastated Japan, people responded compassionately from every sector of society. In these types of disasters, our government sends federal troops and civilian experts to assist with search and recovery efforts. Red Cross and other emergency-assistance organizations jump into action. The media brings the devastation into every living room and provides information on donating to responsible nonprofit groups mobilizing to address the crisis. America is in the forefront of generosity when it comes to extending lifesaving assistance in times of calamity. It is a cultural characteristic that should make us proud.

But our compassionate instinct has a serious shortcoming. Our memory is short when recovery is long. We respond with immediacy to desperate circumstances but often are unable to shift from crisis relief to the more complex work of long-term development. Consequently, aid agencies tend to prolong the "emergency" status of a crisis when a rebuilding strategy should be well under way.

Thus, in 2011, six years after Hurricane Katrina struck New Orleans and long after the city should have shifted to long-term development projects, churches and mission organizations still "market" the crisis and volunteers continue to flow into the city by the thousands, distributing free food and clothing to "victims." When relief does not transition to development in a timely way, compassion becomes toxic.

Not all charity is misspent. There are many stellar examples of organizations, large and small, getting it right. The U.S. government's Millennium Challenge Corporation (MCC) now focuses not merely on dollars invested in developing countries but on the lasting and meaningful changes that result from those investments. Smart investments call for partnerships with countries willing to help themselves, willing to stand up to corruption, and willing to assume accountability for results delivered from each and every investment in their development. In Honduras MCC is investing in agricultural training and infrastructure improvements (roads, bridges) that enable farmers to grow higher-yield crops and transport them efficiently to market. The net result is sustainable economic growth.

Food Security for America, a fledgling nonprofit based in Atlanta, assists churches and other community groups in establishing food co-ops, replacing food pantries that offer free food at the price of recipients' dignity. Food Security organizes food "buying clubs" that leverage the $3 biweekly dues of each low-income member to purchase $30 worth of surplus food.

THIS NATIONAL TOXIC-CHARITY SCANDAL can be reversed if we begin now to take preemptive action to change the compassion industry before it becomes discredited as a national embarrassment. I have seen that such change can happen. In this book I would like to offer basic operating principles that distinguish wise and prudent charitable efforts from the destructive do-gooder practices currently dominating the compassion industry. After describing the problem and hearing stories of people who are modeling solutions, my goal is to provide for caring people a checklist of criteria they can use to determine which actions they should undertake when they want to help others. Perhaps, like the medical profession's Hippocratic Oath, the charity profession will adopt an "Oath for Compassionate Service" to guide us toward providing responsible and effective aid.

These well-tested principles, applied to service work, point individuals and organizations toward practices and partnerships that empower those we wish to assist. You will see them come into play throughout this book—either as models of what we might accomplish or, in their absence, in the stories of where we go wrong.

## *The Oath for Compassionate Service*

- Never do for the poor what they have (or could have) the capacity to do for themselves.

- Limit one-way giving to emergency situations.

- Strive to empower the poor through employment, lending, and investing, using grants sparingly to reinforce achievements.

- Subordinate self-interests to the needs of those being served.

- Listen closely to those you seek to help, especially to what is not being said—unspoken feelings may contain essential clues to effective service.

- Above all, do no harm.

This book explores these principles alongside practical case studies to examine how we practice charity. It takes a candid and sometimes critical look behind the scenes at the unintended harm inflicted by our kindness. My hope is that the following chapters will point the way toward more careful and effective directives for our compassion, to the end that the interactions between the rich and poor may be redemptive—never toxic—for either group.

The current energy driving human compassion is at an all-time high. Rightly deployed, it can move intractable societal problems toward lasting solutions. Rechanneling this awesome force away from toxic activities and into transformative outcomes is not an unrealistic goal. I have witnessed it on a small scale and know it can be done. I believe such a shift is possible on a much broader scale as well. I trust you will agree by the end of this book that we have good reason for hope.

## CHAPTER TWO

# *The Problem with Good Intentions*

WHO WOULD FAULT THE MOTIVATION of compassionate people to help those in need? Certainly not I. It is not motivation, however, that we are questioning but rather the unintended consequences of rightly motivated efforts. Negative outcomes seldom make it into the inspiring reports of service projects and mission trips. This chapter looks behind the scenes at some of the unreported aspects of service.

With enthusiasm and energy my Presbyterian church missions team laid the groundwork for a partnership with a remote Honduran village. A bishop in that region had told us of their desperate need—an isolated people struggling with daily survival needs. Church leaders determined that this would be more than a ten-day service trip. They would make a long-term commitment to this village, build friendships and trust over time, have a true partnership. This would be both a sensitive and responsible investment of time and resources.

On the initial visit one need became obvious. Water. The village women had to carry water from a supply source miles away, spending hours each day trudging in the oppressive heat. The church could do something about that and had connections with well-drilling engineers. The church also had money to cover the costs. This was a desperate need that could be addressed immediately. And the church did so.

When the first water was pumped to the surface and villagers filled their jugs with cool, pure water, there was a great celebration. There were cheers and hugs of joy and many *"gracias, señors."* We had changed these people's lives.

The following year, however, as the church's returning missioners rumbled up the dusty road toward the village, they observed women carrying water jugs as they had done before. Arriving at the village, the team saw that the well was idle. The pump had broken down, and there was no way to draw precious water to the surface. The ministry team knew what they had to do. They repaired the pump. Soon water was flowing in the village once more.

But by the time the team returned the following year, the pump had broken down yet again. And women resumed their toilsome treks. This happened year after year. The village simply waited until their benefactors returned to fix *their* well.

Another remote Central American village had a similar need for water. They, too, were blessed with a partner from the United States. But this Nicaraguan village, unlike the Honduran village, received a mission partner with an altogether different approach to serving.

Opportunity International, a Chicago-based microlending organization, commissioned a community developer to assist the residents in creating a plan for their much-needed well. She assisted them in finding information on drilling and material costs. She helped them formulate a budget and a rudimentary business plan. She arranged for a loan conditional upon villagers' investing their own money from their meager savings. Then she connected them with a reliable Nicaraguan engineer and helped them organize a water commission to set fees, collect water bills, manage finances, and maintain their new utility.

Village men provided all the labor, digging trenches, laying water lines, and setting 220 water meters. When the pump was switched on and water surged to the homes, the village erupted with pride. Their water supply, they soon learned, was abundant—sufficient to allow them to sell water to the local government school and negotiate supplying an adjacent village. They now *owned* and *managed* a wealth-producing asset.

## The Short-Term Service Industry

ACROSS THE SPAN OF four decades I have observed many well-resourced, well-intentioned people attempting to help the poor. I have been among them. My church has been among them. Most of the time, these efforts have produced little lasting benefit for those "served," with a few notable exceptions.

For the most part, when those of us who serve are candid, we admit an uneasiness in our viscera, a largely unspoken concern that our helping might not be accomplishing what we had hoped. This is especially true when it comes to the now-routine practice of sending groups of youth or adults to do service projects.

Critics of short-term trips often point to the make-work nature of many of these service trips. They point to projects like the wall built on an orphanage soccer field in Brazil that had to be torn down after the visitors left. Or the church in Mexico that was painted six times during one summer by six different mission groups. Or the church in Ecuador built by volunteers that was never used as a church because the community had no need for it.

A March 18, 2008 article in *USA Today*, "Christian students get immersed in lives of the poor," reported that Princeton University conducted a study that found 1.6 million American church members took mission trips abroad in 2005—an average of eight days long—at a cost of $2.4 billion. And the number has grown every year since. "Religious tourism," as some call it, has become a growth industry. The web is full of agencies (denominational and parachurch, college, and service organizations) ready to connect service groups and church groups to a "meaningful experience" in an exotic location rife with human need. The Bahamas, it is estimated, annually receives one short-term missionary for every fifteen residents.

Yes, many of our motives are noble. We want to invest in the lives of others. We want to expose youth and adults to the needs of a hurting world. We want to engage people in life-changing experiences. Some of us are motivated by the teachings of Jesus—to clothe the naked, feed the hungry, and show compassion to the oppressed.

Often, though, we miss the big picture because we view aid through the narrow lens of the needs of *our* organization or church—focusing on what will benefit *our* team the most—and neglecting the best interests of those we would serve.

Even when we believe that serving others will at the very least change *us*, early research by Kurt Ver Beek of Calvin College and Robert Priest of Trinity Evangelical Divinity School suggests that service projects and mission trips *do not effect lasting* change. Within six to eight weeks after a mission trip, most short-term mission-trippers return to the same assumptions and behaviors they had prior to the trip.

Contrary to popular belief, most mission trips and service projects *do not:*

- empower those being served
- engender healthy cross-cultural relationships
- improve local quality of life
- relieve poverty

- change the lives of participants

- increase support for long-term mission work

Contrary to popular belief, most mission trips and service projects *do:*

- weaken those being served

- foster dishonest relationships

- erode recipients' work ethic

- deepen dependency

Some Christians argue that short-term service trips whet the appetite for long-term mission involvement. Research, however, does not support this claim. In spite of the moving testimonies of "life-changing experiences" by returning short-termers and the occasional example of full-time missionaries who point to a mission trip as the catalyst for their calling, there is no evidence that missions as a whole has benefited from the rise in short-term service.

If we listen to those on the receiving end of these service projects, we see a different picture emerge. Most work done by volunteers could be better done by locals in less time and with better results. The president of a struggling seminary in Cuba confided in me the conflict she felt hosting U.S. volunteers. A new group of twenty youth and adults had just arrived, eager to lay tile in a new dormitory addition. Not one volunteer had experience in tile work, but the local supervisor remained patient. No matter that some of the grout lines were crooked and the tile had to be reset. No matter that skilled tile layers sat outside the seminary gates, waiting to see if there would be any work left for them after the volunteers left. These volunteers had paid good money to come all the way from the States, and they were expecting to do "meaningful" work.

The seminary president saw to it that kitchen staff prepared plenty of food the Americans would like. She scheduled various faculty members to arrange lodging, offer presentations, and conduct tours. She had all the materials and supervisors lined up for the work. But what she could not do, would not do, was tell her eager, naive servant-volunteers that all this was a gross misappropriation of resources. To do so would almost certainly have cut off the support from this church's missions budget. And this her struggling seminary could not afford to have happen. Oh, what she could have done with the nearly $30,000 this group was spending on this trip! Still, the church's forthcoming, smaller donation for the true needs of the seminary was essential to their continuing work.

Anyone with a business background (or even street smarts) would agree that the amount spent on service trips is extravagant when compared to the monetary value of the actual work done. But when people with business backgrounds enter service work, they repeatedly fail to bring with them their common sense and business acumen, defaulting to traditional charity models. They would not put up with this kind of return on investment in their professional lives. Otherwise, they would see what should be obvious: if the money spent on travel, lodging, food, and staff time were directly invested in the people being served, far more could be accomplished with greater effectiveness.

## Ministry Entrepreneurs

OF COURSE, ALL CHARITABLE activities cannot be painted with the same critical brush. Some groups accomplish amazing results and work efficiency. Opportunity International, for example, invests in poverty-stricken populations through micro-loans to help them build their small, life-sustaining businesses. But responsible development efforts such as these are sometimes thwarted by well-meaning missioners who have little understanding of the negative impacts of their good deeds. Consider the following dilemma currently playing out in Nicaragua.

Microlending offers small loans to peasants in underdeveloped countries to assist them in growing their grass-roots businesses. Like $50 to a woman in Nicaragua who makes hand-stitched baby clothes so she can buy a treadle sewing machine. Or $100 to a woman to enlarge her produce stand and expand her selection at the local village market. Micro-loans at modest interest rates counteract the exploitation of loan sharks and enable the poorest of the culture to take small, steady steps toward economic health.

And the repayment rate is amazingly high. Many micro-finance organizations say their default rate is less than 5 percent. In Nicaragua, for example, Opportunity International (one of its most effective microlenders, who worked with the local community to partner the well project) claimed 98 percent repayment among its thirty-four thousand borrowers scattered throughout the cities and rural villages of that country. Through the establishment of "trust groups"—small clusters of twenty to thirty neighbors, all of whom run tiny businesses—borrowers agree to provide accountability and support for one another. Trust-group members, mostly women, select from among themselves who should receive the first loan and collectively guarantee its repayment. Over time all the members of the trust group receive loans and, with positive credit histories building, the frequency and size of their loans increase. Opportunity International requires each borrower to establish a savings account. Peasants in Nicaragua have accumulated more than $1 million in private savings—a safety net for emergencies, equity for home improvements, or funds for their children's education.

"And how does the church fit into this?" I asked Juan Ulloa, Opportunity International's Nicaragua director, on a recent visit to that country. Juan is a small, soft-spoken man whose vision propelled this poorest of Central American countries into becoming an international model of microenterprise excellence. As a banker-turned-minister, Juan successfully combined marketplace skills and theological training into a ministry that ignited hope among many thousands of desperately poor Nicaraguans. For Juan, this work was more than economic relief—it was the embodiment of Christ's love for the poor. I had to agree, witnessing firsthand the proud faces of peasants reading scripture together in clearings under the canopy of squat shade trees, collecting their weekly payments and savings deposits from one another, and praying together for strength, for success in their little businesses, and for wisdom to deal with village problems.

Juan tried to be diplomatic in responding to my question about the church's involvement with the microlending model. Faint praise indirectly revealed the truth. But finally, after my continuous probing, Juan admitted that many growing Nicaraguan churches were active in their evangelism efforts—and that was good, he added—but they did little to assist their converts in the struggles of their daily lives. They seemed more concerned about saving souls than saving people. The biggest problem, however, was with those churches that have church partners from the United States. And here Juan's expression became very intense. "They destroy the initiative of my people."

He described whole regions of the country where microlending was virtually nonexistent, areas where church partnerships were concentrated. "People say 'Why should we borrow money when the churches give it to us?'"

Juan went on to describe how entrepreneurship declines as dollars and free resources flood in, how people become conditioned to wait for the next mission group to arrive instead of building their businesses through their own efforts. He talked about how dignity is eroded as people come to view themselves as charity cases for wealthy visitors, how they pose with smiling faces for pictures to be taken back for the marketing of the next group. "They are turning my people into beggars," Juan said, now with full emotion.

And what peasant scratching out a bare existence can refuse suitcases bulging with new clothing for his families?

What struggling pastor can resist the temptation to accept a steady salary and generous church income in exchange for hosting visitors, organizing volunteer work, and staffing funded programs?

What village would borrow money to dig a well or buy books for their school library or save money to build a church if these things were provided for them free of charge?

If all they were required to do was make a wish list, show up for the schedule arranged by the donors, and smile graciously until their benefactors head back home, who would blame them for accepting easy charity?

But Juan did not blame them for becoming beggars. He faulted the affluent, well-meaning U.S. churches for their unexamined generosity. His accusations, now pouring forth with considerable force, were directed at the naive "vacationaries" spending millions of dollars traveling to his country, creating a welfare economy that deprives people of the pride of their own accomplishments—all in the name of Christian service.

But it's not only church-based groups that bring toxic charity and use obsolete service models. Those in business, law, engineering, the sciences, and local government also seem oblivious to their default charity mode when they do philanthropic work—even though our nation rejected this type of charity with the passage of the Welfare Reform Act of 1996. As a country, we understand that welfare creates unhealthy dependency, that it erodes the work ethic, that it cannot elevate people out of poverty. Yet we continue to perpetuate ill-thought-through models when we "invest" in service work. Take the story of Billy Mitchell.

### Bad Business Equals Bad Ministry

POWERFUL PEOPLE OFFERING SELFLESS support to the powerless. No thought of repayment. No ulterior motive. Charity work with no strings attached. Seems so noble, so Christian.

That's how Atlanta real-estate developer Billy Mitchell attempted to invest when he volunteered to organize a new community-development corporation to revitalize the long-neglected inner-city neighborhood of Summerhill. A man who had done well in the city wanted to find ways to give back. And he believed that caring for the poor is important to God. So Billy responded from his heart to the appeal of community leaders to help turn their devastated neighborhood around.

As Billy understood it, bringing a volunteer spirit and

service-oriented heart to investing meant listening carefully to the needs and desires of Summerhill residents, then jumping into action on their behalf. The biggest problem, they said, was housing. Their neighborhood was in disarray—streets lined with hundreds of dilapidated rental houses, entire blocks blighted by scores of vacant, trash-strewn lots. If it were ever to be a healthy place for children to grow up, a place with safe streets and thriving businesses, new home-owning neighbors would have to be attracted back. Such a desire might well have been idle fantasy were it not for the fact that the Olympic Summer Games were coming to Atlanta and Summerhill was right in the path. Billy immediately saw the once-in-a-lifetime opportunity.

In order to transform the neighborhood, a nonprofit community-development corporation (CDC) would have to be formed. It would require a blue-ribbon board with all the necessary skills to negotiate complex property deals, secure millions in funding, and manage dozens of projects simultaneously. One concern, however, was that such a high-powered group might easily steamroll right over community leadership. And this mission was about investing in the community, not real-estate conquest. So the decision was made to subordinate the new CDC to the neighborhood association, making it a wholly owned subsidiary of the community. The board and staff of the new CDC would serve at the pleasure of the community and implement the community-defined vision. It all seemed so right. So just.

In the spirit of serving the community, Billy and the board launched into multi-million-dollar real-estate acquisitions, secured millions in loans and foundation grants, attracted large corporate investors, and negotiated Olympics-related deals— all to benefit the community. It was stimulating work made even more rewarding because of its noble purpose. A vacant 840-bed hotel was purchased to be converted to student housing. Blocks of land were cleared, and rows of attractive new homes sprung out of the ground. A public-housing project was transformed and private management hired. The dreams of a forgotten neighborhood were at long last becoming reality.

One big flaw in the strategy, however, proved fatal. In putting together complex, big-dollar real-estate deals, Billy and his capable cadre of prominent business leaders failed to establish adequate guarantees and contingencies to cover the substantial loans and investments. They would never have taken unsecured risks in their corporate business dealings. But because this was all pro bono—for the good of the community— they entered into agreements based upon goodwill rather than good business sense.

And goodwill did carry the mission forward—for a time. Until a disgruntled pro bono attorney got upset when another legal firm scooped up some fees he was entitled to. The project turned ugly. The angry "advocate for the community" launched a personal vendetta against the CDC board, turning the community leaders against the volunteers doing all the heavy lifting. In the mayhem that ensued, Billy was fired, other board members resigned, and law suits were filed. It was like rats jumping off a sinking ship.

Overnight, the vision was dead in the water.

The corporation collapsed, creditors scrambled for whatever they could salvage, and what began as an inspiring vision ended as a devastating debacle. Race relations took a severe blow. Old stereotypes resurfaced as angry community residents exchanged hot words with their bewildered and perplexed would-be benefactors. Fifteen years later Summerhill remains a rudderless neighborhood that no one in the city wants to touch.

Summerhill needed true friends and partners, not softhearted volunteers, friends good enough to clearly define roles and expectations, partners with whom to negotiate responsible if/then contingencies. The board's decision to subordinate its control to the political whims of the community and surrender its ability to deliver on commitments was not only bad business, it was ethically questionable. If Summerhill taught us anything, it was that no-strings-attached service needs some strings attached.

Unselfish self-investment may be freely offered with no expectation of repayment. It may not seek credit. It may even be anonymous. But unselfish investment should:

- never be mindless
- never be irresponsible
- always calculate the cost

- always consider the outcome
- always be a partnership

## Money and Partnership

IN THE FOLLOWING STORY, Ron Nikkel, president of Prison Fellowship International, describes the challenges he encountered moving from a traditional charity model to a partnership of international members, putting policies in place that invest in healthy, long-term relationships.

Following the 1976 founding of Prison Fellowship in the USA by Chuck Colson, there was a great deal of interest among prison chaplains and prison volunteers around the world. The stature of prison ministry was raised to a new level by Colson's White House-to-jailhouse conversion story, and many were intrigued by the idea of starting a Prison Fellowship in their own countries. Along with this came the inevitable requests for assistance, if not outright support—at least start-up grants.

Initially, that is exactly what Prison Fellowship (PF) did. By the time I joined Prison Fellowship International, the relationship between the PF organizations in other countries that had been funded and PF in the United States were already contentious. PF in England and Canada had received start-up grants, but now they were demanding additional funding to keep them going—and if not a grant, then a loan. Money became a political problem in the relationships. On the one hand the recipients felt manipulated anytime they felt or suspected that we were in any way being directive. On the other hand we felt that we had learned a few things in prison ministry and simply wanted to share those best practices with them.

It did not take me long to realize that the development of a healthy international organization had to be built on relationships in which each national organization was an equal partner and participated on an equal basis. We stopped the grants and loans, instead requiring that every national PF ministry be responsible for its own funding. And not only that—each national PF was required to pay a standard percentage of their income to the PF International association as a membership fee. Membership would be voluntary, and any PF organization could opt out at any time, but in doing so, it would lose its license to use the PF name.

On the basis of membership fees, PF International began to provide training, consultation, and other membership services to its member organizations. In thirty years the number of national PF organizations around the world grew from 5 to 117.

Not a single one of these ministries receives grants

or loans for start-up or for ongoing operations. Today national PF ministries as diverse as PF Nepal, PF Benin, PF Venezuela, and PF Papua New Guinea raise their own funds and contribute their annual membership fees for the support and extension of the ministry worldwide.

Sooner or later most PF ministries realize that they are working with a population of people that is often the poorest of the poor. Not only are they poor and often marginalized to begin with, but the reality is that in countries with high unemployment it is virtually impossible for a person with a prison record to get a job. In response, a number of PF organizations have learned not to provide ex-prisoners with the financial assistance they inevitably ask for. Instead, these PF groups have begun providing prisoners and ex-prisoners with skills training and often repayable microloans and business mentoring to enable them to create their own small businesses—whether tailoring service, motorcycle repair, landscaping, fruit and vegetable stands, pedicabs, barbering, and so forth, in order to become self-supporting.

Again and again we are finding that when it comes to global needs in organizational development and human development, the granting of money creates dependence and conflict, not independence and respect. By changing the equation to other means of exchange, we find that we are empowering people based on shared responsibility, mutual support, and accountability.

Stories like these line the pages of this book. Some critically explore what happens at ground level when caring people lead with their hearts but ignore checks on their intellect. Through case studies, the following chapters reflect on the unsettling reality of charity work. Yet also woven throughout this book are informative glimpses into the private struggles and victories of those who attempt to navigate their churches or organizations away from traditional "doing for" the poor models toward a "doing with" paradigm. Here, you will meet thoughtful, courageous people who risked examining their current methods of service and forged ahead to develop enlightened new technologies of compassion. I hope you will find sufficient encouragement in these pages to inspire new models of caring.

# CHAPTER THREE

## The Anatomy of Giving

GIVING IS NO SIMPLE MATTER, not if giving is to be ultimately redemptive. And there are no cookie-cutter formulas for getting it right. Theologians and social practitioners, while agreeing on the value of generosity, differ widely in their opinions about its application. The struggle to find the optimal path is exemplified in the following accounts.

It was my first Christmas living in the inner city, the first time I had the luxury of relaxing on a Christmas Eve in the living room of a low-income family. Usually I was rushing back and forth from the suburbs with vanloads of presents and food for the poor, organizing toy parties, coordinating adopt-a-family gift deliveries. This year was different. I was no longer a commuter. I was a neighbor.

My decision to live in the city came after a decade of counseling struggling inner-city families. Over time it became apparent that the best chance for these families to build hopeful futures lay in effecting change from within their neighborhoods. When our organization, Focused Community Strategies, decided to direct the work more locally, several of our staff committed themselves to move in, become neighbors, and join the community in this transformational effort.

That's why Christmas Eve of '81 I celebrated the season as a newcomer to this urban neighborhood, sipping coffee with one of my new neighbors.

Bare floors were swept clean, and clutter was picked up. The smell of Pine-Sol hung in the air. Front windows reflected the light from two plastic candles. A small artificial tree on a corner table blinked with a single strand of colored lights. The children, antsy with anticipation, paced from window to window, waiting for Santa's helpers to arrive.

When the knock finally came on their front door, their mom greeted the visitors—a well-dressed family with young children—and invited them to step inside. A nervous smile concealed her embarrassment as she graciously accepted armfuls of neatly wrapped gifts. In the commotion, no one noticed that the children's father had quietly slipped out of the room— no one but their mom.

Not until the guests were gone and the children had torn through the wrappings to the treasures inside did one of the little ones ask where their father was. No one questioned the mother's response that he had to go to the store. But after organizing these kinds of Christmas charity events for years, I was witnessing a side I had never noticed before: how a father is emasculated in his own home in front of his wife and children for not being able to provide presents for his family, how a wife is forced to shield her children from their father's embarrassment, how children get the message that the "good stuff" comes from rich people out there and it is free.

Only after becoming a neighbor was I able to see what we had done. Christmas Eve in that living room, I became painfully aware that not all charity is good charity.

Even the most kindhearted, rightly motivated giving—as innocent as giving Christmas toys to needy children—can exact an unintended toll on a parent's dignity. Inadvertently I had done just that. Not just this time but many times.

*This kind of charity has to stop,* I vowed. The cost was just too great, the emotional pain too severe. There had to be a better way.

So much of our holiday season, from Thanksgiving till Christmas, is consumed with giving—turkeys distributed by the score, free feasts in the church fellowship hall, heaping food baskets for seniors, Santa parties for kids. Giving is supposed to be a joyous process, but throughout our various giving activities I had overlooked the darker side. Emotional price tags were attached to each of these charitable events. I thought, too, about our church clothes closet and food pantry—did those have the same issues at play?

About that time I happened across the devastating words

written by Jacques Ellul, a French philosopher and lay theologian, in *Money and Power:*

> It is important that giving be truly free. It must never degenerate into charity, in the pejorative sense. Almsgiving is Mammon's perversion of giving. It affirms the superiority of the giver, who thus gains a point on the recipient, binds him, demands gratitude, humiliates him and reduces him to a lower state than he had before.

Charity a perversion? Toxic? That thought clung to me for weeks. Every interaction with low-income neighbors became suspect. I began studying the facial expressions of those I ushered into our church clothes closet. I noticed how seldom recipients gave me direct eye contact. I watched body language as I handed out boxes of groceries from our food pantry—head and shoulders bent slightly forward, self-effacing smiles, meek "thank-yous." I observed, too, how quickly recipients' response to charity devolved from gratitude to expectation to entitlement.

In moments of silent introspection, I observed my part in the anatomy of giving: I expected gratitude in exchange for my free gifts. I actually enjoyed occupying the superior position of giver (though I covered it carefully with a facade of humility). I noted a hidden irritation at those who voiced their annoyance when free food stocks ran low. I grew weary of filtering through half-truths and manipulative ploys as I sought to equitably dispense resources. This thorough look at the anatomy of my charity eventually exposed an unhealthy culture of dependency.

With the research intensity of a Louis Pasteur searching for a causal relationship between germs and disease, I examined broader aspects of charity under the microscope of my new awareness. I discovered that the toxins deforming relationships were not confined to our organization or the neighborhood I served. Everywhere I looked, I observed the same patterns, from overseas church mission trips to the inner-city service projects of campus organizations. Wherever there was sustained one-way giving, unwholesome dynamics and pathologies festered under the cover of kindheartedness.

Since that 1981 Christmas Eve, it has baffled me that in a global communication era no watchdog organization warns of the dangers of charity, especially given the growth and popularity of this industry. Now, everyone is getting in on the charity train, from rock groups to youth groups, from TV celebrities to elementary-school children, from Fortune 500 corporations to campus fraternities. And across the board the benevolence business is almost entirely unexamined.

Doing *for* rather than doing *with* those in need is the norm. Add to it the combination of patronizing pity and unintended superiority, and charity becomes toxic.

BUT ROCK STARS AND church groups are not the only ones leading with their hearts rather than sound reason and intellect. Governments and world leaders are plagued by similar blind spots.

Take Haiti, for example. No other country in the Western Hemisphere has received more charitable aid and services from governments and nonprofits. Yet its poverty and dysfunction continue to deepen.

During the four decades prior to the devastating earthquake of January 2010, $8.3 billion in foreign aid flowed into Haiti. Yet the country has ended up 25 percent poorer than before the aid began. The current earthquake tragedy has ballooned additional aid commitments by another $9 billion from thirty-nine countries. But the prognosis for sustained improvement is no better today. "The problem is not goodwill," says anthropologist Timothy Schwartz, longtime Haiti resident who emailed from the midst of the earthquake devastation. "I don't even think the problem is resources. . . . The big problem is lack of accountability, lack of a mechanism to pressure aid agencies into effective, long-term development." Schwartz has witnessed it all firsthand.

Decades of free aid from well-meaning benefactors has produced an entitlement mentality and eroded a spirit of entrepreneurship and self-sufficiency. The outpouring of more aid, though necessary to preserve life in a time of disaster, is ultimately worsening the underlying problem. Humanitarian responses unaccompanied by disciplined development strategies become a curse on a country. Dambisa Moyo, in her best-selling exposé, *Dead Aid*, writes about assistance to her native

Africa: "The reality is aid has helped make the poor poorer and growth slower. Aid has been, and continues to be, an unmitigated political, economic and humanitarian disaster for most parts of the developing world."

If giving our resources hurts the poor as often as (or even more often than) it helps, how are we to be responsible stewards of resources? From my painful Christmas Eve drama until the present, this question has been my persistent companion.

## *Parity vs. Charity*

FOR THREE DECADES NOW I have experimented, both in the living laboratory of my urban community and in Third-World settings, with methods to minimize the toxins and foster health in the relationships between the haves and have-lesses.

It is delicate work, I have found, establishing authentic parity between people of unequal power. But relationships built on reciprocal exchange (what I call holistic compassion) make this possible. Thrift stores, unlike free-clothes closets, are legitimate businesses that *need* customers to pay the light bill and make weekly payroll. And unlike clothes closets that place limits on the number of visits and garments a recipient is allowed, a thrift store relies on attracting paying customers to purchase as many clothes as they are able. When the customer is necessary to ensure the business's survival, there is equity of power. And parity is the higher form of charity.

The challenge for those of us in service work is to redirect traditional methods of charity into systems of genuine exchange. In our community there was no small amount of grumbling over our decision to close down the church clothes closet and open the nonprofit Family Store. Those forfeiting significant portions of their dignity for the addiction of welfare (religious or otherwise) do not easily part with this dependency.

We discovered it is more difficult to detoxify pathological relationships than to build new, healthy, reciprocal relationships between the rich and poor. But you have to start somewhere. Several things, however, eased neighbors' withdrawal from our free clothing program. Seeing former clothes-closet recipients working as paid employees behind the counter was a hopeful sign. Discovering bargains generates excitement—universally. And being greeted as valued customers, not charity cases, affirmed self-esteem. Within a year most forgot that we once even had a church clothes closet.

The following Christmas we terminated our adopt-a-family gift-giving program. When well-resourced families called to contribute to a family, we asked if they would be willing to give an extra gift that year—the gift of dignity to the dads. Instead of delivering toys directly to the homes of the poor, donors were directed to bring unwrapped gifts to the Family Store where a large section was decorated as The Old Toy Shop. A bargain price was placed on each toy, and parents from the neighborhood were invited to come shopping for the special gifts sure to delight their children. Those who had no money were able to work at the store, earning what they needed for their purchases. In this way parents in the city experienced the same joy on Christmas morning as most other parents across the nation—seeing their children opening gifts they had purchased through the efforts of their own hands.

That second Christmas our predictions proved spot-on: our low-income neighbors would much rather work to purchase gifts for their children than stand in free-toy lines with their "proof of poverty" identification.

### When Justice and Mercy Meet

COMPASSION IS A DANGEROUS thing. It can open a person to all manner of risks. It causes reasonable people to make extravagant heart decisions, from spending untold hours collecting supplies to assist flood victims, to journeying into harm's way to feed starving refugees. Some have even left successful careers, devoting themselves to a cause that gripped their hearts.

Compassion is a powerful force, a stamp of the divine nature within our spirits. It lies within us all—from tender child to hardened criminal—waiting for the right trigger to set it off: a bird with a broken wing, a lonely widow whose family and friends have moved on, a child orphaned by a terrorist car bomb.

For me it was fatherless boys growing up on city streets with little chance of escaping the deadly undertow. So strong was that force within me that it caused me to leave a budding business career, depart secure surroundings, and move with my family into the inner city.

Compassion beckons us into unexplored territory. Often it ushers us into a world of pressing human need—the destitute needing food and clothes, the homeless needing shelter, the refugee needing a connected friend. My focus became attention-starved boys. I forged friendships with them through all sorts of testosterone-charged activities—minibiking, spelunking, deep-sea fishing—along with enticing rewards for good grades and staying out of trouble. Friendship with them was the medium for showing them they were valued and loved by a God who care-fully created them.

Building relationships with street kids seemed so right and yielded so many positive changes, until young boys became young men and faced survival on their own. The need for immediate cash took precedence over school attendance. Basketball and outdoor adventure trips did little to enhance their earning capacity. Bible studies did not get them jobs. I watched helplessly as one by one my young friends were pulled under by the survival ethic of the street. Mercy ministry alone, as some call it, is insufficient.

Mercy is a force that compels us to acts of compassion. But in time mercy will collide with an ominous, opposing force. Injustice. Against this dark and overpowering force, acts of mercy can seem meager. What good is a sandwich and a cup of soup when a severe addiction has control of a man's life? Or a night in a shelter for a young woman who must sell her body to feed her child?

Perhaps that is why the Bible places equal emphasis on both mercy and justice. The ancient prophet Micah succinctly summarizes God's design: "He has shown you, O mortal, what is good. And what does the LORD require of you? To act justly and to love mercy and to walk humbly with your God" (6:8, NIV).

*Act justly.* Justice is "fairness or reasonableness, especially in the way people are treated or decisions are made."

*Love mercy.* Mercy is "compassion, kindness, or forgiveness shown especially to someone over whom a person has power."

Twinned together, these commands lead us to holistic involvement. Divorced, they become deformed. Mercy without justice degenerates into dependency and entitlement, preserving the power of the giver over the recipient. Justice without mercy is cold and impersonal, more concerned about rights than relationships. The addict needs both food and treatment. The young woman needs both a safe place to sleep and a way out of her entrapping lifestyle. Street kids need both friendship and jobs.

Mercy combined with justice creates:

- immediate care with a future plan
- emergency relief and responsible development

- short-term intervention and long-term involvement
- heart responses and engaged minds

Mercy is a door, an opening, an invitation to touch a life, to make a difference. But it is not a destination. Those of us who get stuck in mercy ministry find ourselves growing impatient with the recipients of our kindness, wondering why they don't help themselves more, feeling a growing discomfort with the half truths they tell us to justify their persistent returns for more handouts. Mercy that doesn't move intentionally in the direction of development (justice) will end up doing more harm than good—to both giver and recipient.

Mercy is also a portal through which we glimpse the heart of God. The tug on our heartstrings draws us in. But soon we encounter brokenness so overwhelming that neither tender heart nor inventive problem solver feels up to the task. Our solutions fall short. Pathologies are too deep, poverty too entrenched. And we descend into our own poverty, a poverty of spirit, a crisis of confidence in our own abilities to rescue. And, like the broken, we find ourselves calling out to God for answers. When our best efforts have failed us, we are left with nothing to cling to but frail faith.

In a strange twist of divine irony, those who would extend mercy discover that they themselves are in need of mercy. Out of our own need, we are readied for service that is both humble and wise.

## What About the Homeless?

So, WHAT DOES IT look like in our day-to-day lives, to bring mercy and justice together? One of the most pressing, visible, daily issues that as a nation confronts us is homelessness. A recent *USA Today* study estimates that one in every one hundred Americans goes homeless at some point during the year. And in a troubled economy, that number grows. For those of us who frequently encounter the street-corner needy, how do we discriminate between panhandlers making a living through the homeless label and the desperate person temporarily down on his or her luck? Are we offering justice to the homeless man by dropping change into his empty Dunkin' Donuts cup? The subject came up recently when I was having breakfast with my good friend John.

John stared intently at me over the steam of our first cup of breakfast coffee. "There's something I'd like your opinion on"—not his usual lighthearted banter that began our monthly breakfast time. "What am I supposed to do with all these people who want something from me?" he asked.

John had money, and lots of people knew it. He had read Jesus's directive to give to anyone who asks—totally impractical, it seemed to him. He could handle the calls and letters requesting money, he said. It was the pleading expressions on the faces: the father whose family was about to be put out on the street unless he came up with rent money, the young woman at the gas station who needed just $27.15 to get her car out of repair to return home to Alabama, the homeless man outside of church who needed a dollar for food.

Those who know John know he is a generous man. He gives significant sums to missions and makes sure his investments go directly to the causes he has designated, instead of being diverted to overhead and fundraising professionals. He asks for financial statements from the 501(c)(3) organizations he supports. He requests the annual audit report from his church. He wants to be sure his charitable giving is supported by due diligence.

But where there are no records facilitating due diligence, is there any way of knowing that giving isn't simply enabling an addicted person to continue a destructive, irresponsible lifestyle? John couldn't get the words of the Teacher out of his mind: "Whatever you did for one of the least of these . . . you did for me" (Matt. 25:40, NIV).

A lifetime of serving in the city should have fine-tuned my compassion skills, but as I confessed to John, I get as furious as he does when I find out that the young woman at the gas station has used that $27.15 story to con suckers at gas stations all over the city. Could our reluctance to give to a stranger on the street be more than a conditioned reaction reinforced by other cons we have fallen prey to? Could it be a righteous response in our spirits cautioning us to avoid irresponsible giving that harms both recipient and giver?

I wished I could have portrayed more conviction. All I had

to draw upon was four decades of pragmatic trial and error, common sense, and intuition somewhat jaded by too many deceptions. And, of course, the calling that had been my orienting compass.

John's struggle, though intensely personal, was hardly an individual one. People of faith and goodwill all over the world wrestle with the same issue. In a January 2011 *Christianity Today* article the question was posed to three veteran ministry leaders known for their commitment to the poor: Should Christians always give money to street people who ask for it?

"Yes, freely!" answers Gary Hoag, known as the Generosity Monk, whose passionate mission is to encourage Christian generosity. To him it is very clear in scripture: "Freely you have received; freely give" (Matt. 10:8). It is not our place to judge others, to evaluate them as worthy or unworthy of our assistance. God is the judge, not us. What they do with our aid is between them and God. We are to love and give unconditionally.

Andy Bales, CEO of Union Rescue Mission in Los Angeles, sees it differently. "Giving cash to someone in need is the least helpful and most temporary solution and should only be a last resort," he says. His years of experience with street people have taught him that most panhandlers are not really homeless at all. Most are scammers who may collect $300 a day from kindhearted passersby and at the end of the day walk a block or two to their cars and drive home. When people approach Andy for money for food or a place to stay, he gives them his card and invites them to his mission where they can get not only food and shelter but other support as well. Very seldom does he give money, and then only when there are no other alternatives. He refers to the story of the lame man in scripture who asked Peter and John for some money. They offered no money but rather something better—healing. "People experiencing homelessness and poverty need a caring community," Andy says. "People need permanent help in becoming strong. They need a connection with Jesus Christ and a faith community."

"Absolutely not!" says Ron Sider, president of Evangelicals for Social Action and author of *Rich Christians in an Age of Hunger*. A quick donation is cheap love. There is simply no way to tell whether a story is legitimate, or if a person will spend the money on drugs or alcohol. Supporting immorality, laziness, or destructive behavior is simply irresponsible and clearly not a loving act. Scripture demands that we stand on the side of the poor, but it certainly does not tell us to give irresponsibly. Rather than giving money, Sider suggests taking the homeless person to lunch and listening to his story. "People almost always need love even more than money," he says. Generous giving should be directed toward effective, holistic programs equipped to deal with the deeper socioeconomic issues, ministries that share the love of Christ and "truly liberate, empower, and transform."

Always. Sometimes. Never. Three respected Christian leaders, all committed to helping the poor, all relying on the scriptures to guide them, each with distinctly different convictions on how to rightly serve. They take their stands at different points on the charity continuum, from "always give money" to "never give money."

One thing John and I readily *did* agree upon as we sipped our third cup of coffee was the deep sense of satisfaction that registers within us when we give of ourselves to meet a legitimate human need. When we help a frantic child find his mother in a department store or assist a widow by patching a leaking roof, something smiles deep within us. When the need is real and the situation critical, we will gladly sacrifice our time, resources, and even personal safety to rescue someone from trouble. This desire to help echoes the imprint of the Creator on our lives.

And there is something that reacts viscerally in our spirits when we encounter grave injustice. When a confidence man defrauds a widow out of her life savings, or an executive embezzles his employees' hard-earned retirement investments, our outrage at such despicable conduct is also a reflection of the divine imprint.

So why does John feel so guilty when he turns away a beggar holding a sign that says "Homeless, need help, God bless you" when John knows that there is virtually no way to determine that a gift would have a beneficial effect? Why the guilt when John refuses to support the questionable plea of a stranger when he would refuse that same kind of unchecked giving to his own son?

Then John and I broke into laughter, recalling the antics of a couple of homeless guys who sometimes wait in front of our church on Sunday mornings and put the touch on exiting worshippers. Refuse their appeals, and their meek can-you-help-me expressions immediately change into and-you-call-yourself-a-Christian barbs. They know their market. We couldn't decide which emotion was stronger—guilt from refusing to help or anger from being manipulated.

These homeless entrepreneurs have learned through hard experience what relief agencies have known for a long time—pity is a powerful motivator. Portray a picture of desperation, and the human heart instinctively reacts. Too much wretchedness, and people are grossed out; too much hope, and a would-be donor gets away guilt-free. The right mix of misery and hope gets the dollar.

While the comic relief felt good, the disturbing reality brought us back to John's original question.

Don't give because you might be contributing to someone's drug problem? Give because providing a cup of soup and a warm coat might be lifesaving acts? There is no simple or immediate way to discern the right response without a relationship. Offer an honest day's pay for someone to do an honest day's work? Create legitimate exchange between worker and employer, regardless of how he chooses to spend his earnings? Realistically, though, would John take off work to supervise the labor of a homeless person? Better to support a program that is in the business of working with the homeless?

After all the questions, this is the best I could offer John: due diligence. And if you don't have time to invest in forging a trusting relationship, give your money to a ministry that does.

Even so, every once in a while we might feel an inner nudge to stop immediately and help a person, offering food or money or a ride. This may well be the intervention of the divine showing unconditional grace at a critical point in someone's life. Still, there is no way of knowing until the curtain of history is pulled back to reveal the unknowable.

# CHAPTER FOUR

## *Needs vs. Relationships*

CURE WITHOUT CARE IS LIKE a gift given from a cold heart. Charity that does not enhance trusting relationships may not be charity at all. Consider the relational outcomes of the following activities, and judge for yourself which qualify as true charity.

The line begins to form well before eight in the morning, a colorful cross section of humanity—homeless men with graying hair bushing beneath stocking caps, gaunt young women dragging on cigarettes, strong young men leaning nonchalantly against the building, obese women with preschoolers clinging to their dresses, nondescript people dressed in work clothes of various sorts. Soon, though not soon enough for the waiting crowd, the large church doorknob twists. The sound causes an immediate straightening and tightening of the line. The doors swing open, and the impatient stream of humanity surges through, pushing down the hall to the sign-in counter where a well-dressed lady wearing a kindly smile waits to examine IDs, record names and addresses, and issue vouchers. It's Wednesday morning at Old First Church. Time for the free food distribution.

Those familiar with the system know the routine. They have been through this many times. For the newer comers, the rules are posted on the wall. *One visit per month. Must have legitimate ID. One bag per household*—the list goes on. Some recipients play by the rules. Others don't, offering excuses. Still others bring heartrending stories that would cause a lesser-experienced food-pantry manager to bend the rules. But the smiling lady at the sign-in counter has heard it all before. She takes the grumbling, the dejected expressions, the arguments, all in stride and politely points to the posted rules. Some might call her jaded, but in fact she keeps a challenging ministry running efficiently and keeps a consistently positive attitude.

Over time, the smiling lady and those who volunteer with her recognize the faces of regulars, get to know names and their stories. On rare occasions food-pantry workers step out of their roles to help recipients with a personal problem. But that can lead to complications, set a bad precedent. Other recipients take notice and complain of favoritism. Better to stay within the posted guidelines, keep interactions cordial and friendly while avoiding personal involvement.

A few blocks away in the basement of an old brick church, another group of struggling humanity gathers. They assemble as a semiorganized team of food redistributers. They spread out an array of food-bank procurements on folding tables, fill boxes with a balanced assortment, check their list of those who have paid the $3 membership dues, and issue boxes to paid-up members. Fifty households are represented and everyone is engaged.

Some make the run to the food bank. Others do the setup. Some sort and box. Still others are assigned cleanup duty. And there are joint decisions to be made. Who gets the canned hams (not enough this week for every household)? Who can deliver a box to a shut-in member? Should an inactive member be replaced? This is a food-distribution business owned and operated by dues-paying members. This is the Georgia Avenue Food Co-op.

Unlike the food pantry at Old First Church, the Georgia Avenue Food Co-op fosters community. Co-op members (not church volunteers) make and enforce the rules. Co-op members select the food they desire, avoiding the haphazard bring-any-can-on-Sunday food drives.

No giveaway charity here. Co-op members pay their own way. Their $3 semiweekly dues are leveraged into $30 worth of groceries. It's simple: if you don't pay, you don't participate this week. Over time co-op members build friendships, share meals, listen to one another's joys and woes, pray for one another—in essence they become church.

These two versions of food distribution point to a basic principle: sometimes when we work so hard to develop efficient systems to dispense charity, with clearly posted rules, we overlook the costs in human dignity. In doing so, we develop toxic relationships. Even when the toxic nature of the relationship is brought to light, those invested in traditional models of giving resist the call to change.

## Cheap Food

I WON'T MENTION HER name, but you may recognize her. She was one of three dozen church staff and volunteers gathered for an evening meal and discussion around issues of benevolence and service to the poor. I was their invited guest speaker.

When it came time for Q&A, she was the first to speak out. An attractive, well-spoken woman in her forties, she asked me to clarify a statement I made about the damaging effects of giveaway charity. I learned that she was the director of a community food bank—a *co-op* she called it—supported by a number of local churches. During the economic downturn, she said, the number of recipients served by her program had risen dramatically. Her food bank helped people at the basic level of survival, she said, going on to describe in detail the well-coordinated methods of food collection, the computerized systems for keeping track of recipient visits, the monitoring of food quantity outflow.

"So, how could you say that giving food to hungry people could possibly be hurtful?" she asked with great emotion.

Heads bobbed in vigorous assent. I didn't want to insult my audience, obviously vested in the food-pantry program. Nor did I want to encourage a toxifying system of local relationships.

I described how a number of churches had converted their food pantries into food co-ops (not a cooperative giving arrangement among participating churches but a buying co-op of low-income members). I told them about Food Security for America, an Atlanta-based nonprofit that assists churches in establishing these food co-ops (www.gacm.org). I explained how paying into a food-buying collective that yields a purchasing value ten times the amount of each member's bi-weekly contribution brings a genuine sense of personal and community gain. And how a sense of community grows as members work together to supply one another with these basics.

Several faces in the audience began to show a glimmer of interest.

"That might work in a *defined* neighborhood," the attractive lady conceded, "but we serve the entire county. People come from miles away. They're too scattered out to organize food co-ops out where they live."

"Now that *is* a challenge," I admitted. It would require getting out to the poverty pockets, the trailer parks, the low-income apartments where the poor live. It might require partnering with the churches and apartment property managers in lower-income neighborhoods to help set up food cooperatives. It would require a lot of coordinating. And it would mean growing a larger network of relationships. But wouldn't the gains in human dignity and self-esteem be worth the additional effort?

The competent director reassured me, "Our churches really feel good about our cooperative food ministry." The system is efficient, generates compelling stories and statistics, gives regular feedback to donating church members, has controls for hoarding and fraud, and maintains good books. Why wouldn't churches feel good about donating their resources? The food pantry met every traditional charity model requirement: nominal monetary investment, a calendar of regular food drives, sign-up sheets for volunteers, one small rent-free facility, and one paid coordinator. Check. Beyond that, it satisfied a biblical mandate to care for the poor. Check.

"Can we be honest?" I asked, scanned the crowd for at least one or two nods. The director of the charity gave her consent. "Is food the greatest need of the poor in this society? Poor nutrition is certainly a problem, yes, but not starvation." During four decades of urban ministry I could not recall one starving child.

Food in our society is a chronic poverty need, not a life-threatening one. And when we respond to a chronic need as though it were a crisis, we can predict toxic results: dependency, deception, disempowerment.

"But what about those who have lost their jobs? They need support." Absolutely, I agreed. "A job readiness and placement ministry could address that directly." The more I spoke, the

more it was clear that this was not the answer they were looking for. "A jobs program would be good," someone responded,
returning to the original emotional plea, "but what about the
hundreds of needy people standing in long lines for enough
food to feed their families for another day?"

Exasperated, I asked, "Why do we persist in giving away
food when we *know* it fosters dependency?"

"Because it's easier!" the attractive lady blurted out. "It
costs much less in time and money to run a food pantry, and
that's what the churches want!" Her candor stunned all of
us. She was unstoppable. "Churches want their members to
feel good about serving the poor, but no one really wants to
become involved in messy relationships." She spoke the truth
that I had not dared name.

After the meeting, several people came up and asked if I
could meet with their church leadership to discuss changes
in their food-based charity work. I was eager to do so. But,
months later, no one has contacted me. Perhaps someday they
will.

For some reason healthy people with hearts full of compassion forget fundamentals when it comes to building relationships with those they attempt to serve. Forging ahead to meet
a need, we often ignore the basics: mutuality, reciprocity, accountability. In doing so, relationships turn toxic.

### *Need-Based Relationships*

ANN MET JANICE AT a church-run soup kitchen and was immediately drawn to her. Janice's mothering instincts with her two daughters caught Ann's attention. Unlike many of the dejected women who showed up for food, Janice seemed sharp and winsome, with dark penetrating eyes and a bright smile. Her girls were always near her, neatly dressed with hair meticulously braided. Ann sat down at their table and was soon caught up in an engaging conversation.

Janice, it turns out, was staying temporarily in a women's shelter, having lost her job and apartment due to an injury she sustained from a fall. Her unemployment insurance was slow in coming and her savings were quickly depleted. Even with prospects for a new job, her landlord filed for eviction. She had nowhere to store their furniture and clothing so they left with what they could carry. She and her girls had stayed with a friend for several weeks, but the apartment manager there eventually issued a "violation of lease."

Ann was moved to compassion. Here was a good woman, a mother, doing her very best to maintain a semblance of order for herself and her children in a chaotic moment in their lives. What this woman needed was some stability while she got back on her feet. She needed an apartment, some basic furnishings, a supply of food—in short, she needed breathing room so she could make a new start.

Within a day, Ann had secured an apartment for the family. Within the week, Ann's friends had it furnished. One trip to the supermarket stocked the cupboards and refrigerator. Over the next few weeks the relationship between Ann and Janice seemed to deepen. They talked for hours about Janice's past, the abusive marriage she had escaped, her move to Atlanta to start a new life, her accident, how her dreams were dashed in their descent into homelessness.

Janice could not thank Ann enough for intervening at the moment of her deepest despair. It had to be God, she said.

Janice's hopes of getting a new job did not work out as well as expected. When Ann attempted to assist her, the response was polite but less than enthusiastic. It was Janice's responsibility and, as both of them agreed, it might take some time to secure suitable employment. In the meantime, Ann paid for another month's rent, and her friends supplied more food— and some cute clothes for the girls. They all understood it would take time.

Four months passed. Then the Christmas season came. Janice still hadn't landed a job, but a couple of interviews looked promising. Ann's friends were eager to collect gifts for the family to make their Christmas as bright as possible. The relationship between Ann and Janice, however, began to fray. Details about Janice's past, about her friends who were in and out of her apartment, just didn't line up. Janice kept insisting that Ann was her angel, sent by God, and pled with her not to abandon them now. Not at Christmas!

Christmastime revealed, unexpectedly, other pieces of Janice's story—details that she carefully concealed. When some of Ann's friends delivered their gifts, they encountered a houseful of other "angels" loaded down with wonderful, expensive presents for the girls. Hardly the scene of a struggling, single-parent family just weeks out of a homeless shelter. That was the last month that Ann covered the rent.

Relationships built on need are seldom healthy. There is an implicit expectation (at least a hope) that the recipient of charity will use that assistance to better himself. The immediate predicament may pluck at one's heartstrings, but if it persists, the tune in time goes sour. No one wants to support irresponsibility. Or create dependency. Or feel used. Unless the victim of misfortune exerts honest effort to regain self-reliance, the relationship between helper and helpee will tend to deteriorate. At some point accountability is required. The lack of full disclosure opens the door to suspicion and mistrust. Communication becomes strained. The recipient feels controlled by the strings attached by the giver, and the giver feels deceived by the recipient's lack of candor. The relationship eventually dissolves.

Relationships built on need tend to be short-lived. Janice is smart enough to realize that her crisis situation has powerful emotional appeal to tenderhearted benefactors. Her story, accurate in some respects, if properly presented to the right people, will elicit support. Ann and friends were the right people. Janice found it easier to remain in her victim role than to make the hard climb toward self-sufficiency. She sold her story to tenderhearted mothers rather than sell herself to a business-minded employer.

Relationships built on need do not reduce need. Rather, they require more and more need to continue. The ways that victim and rescuer relate become familiar communication paths. The victim brings the dilemma; the rescuer finds the solution. When one problem is solved, another must be presented in order for the relationship to continue. If the victim no longer needs a solution, the rescuer is no longer needed. And the relationship ends or must dramatically change.

## When We Learn to Trust "Them"

TRUST IS THE FOUNDATION of all human relationships. Without trust marriages dissolve, business partnerships collapse, loyalty evaporates. Trust is the bedrock upon which civil society is built. Without it we resort to self-protection, erect defensive walls, remain forever on guard.

Trust is also the essence of faith. We Christians believe in a God we cannot see. We pledge ourselves to a community charged with demonstrating selfless love for one another. The interests of others are to be held above our own. Learning to trust one another, to be trustworthy in our relationships, is the foundation upon which such community flourishes.

But even the church never measures up to these high ideals.

As hard as we try, sometimes we hurt other people. Egos often get in the way. But we continue to aspire to healthy community life.

Given that trust is such a high value for people of faith, one would expect their charity to encourage honest relationships between giver and recipient. In practice, however, rarely are recipients members of the disbursing community in the Western church. And as cordial and as genuinely friendly as givers may be, the poor remain on the outside. Resources are owned by insiders. Rules are devised by those in control.

The giver-recipient relationship is doomed from the start. Such relationships hardly foster trust. Usually they breed resentment. The recipient must figure out the rules of the system, determine the kind of appeal most likely to secure the maximum benefit, learn the language that best matches the dispenser's values, and, above all, be sincere. Half truths are acceptable. Fabrication may be necessary. It doesn't really matter since this is about working a system, not joining a community. Givers, then, must continually tighten the rules, close off loopholes, guard against favoritism, and be ever vigilant to detect manipulation or outright fraud. The system lends itself to adversarial relationships.

If trust is essential for building relationships and making enterprises run effectively, then we have to find a way for outsiders to become insiders. Recipients must become dispensers, authors of the rules, builders of community.

Impossible? Hardly. Take the food co-op at the Georgia

Avenue Church that was mentioned earlier. Members are invited to buy into a "buying club" model in which they assume full responsibility for every aspect of the operation. The church facilitates the process, legitimizes the arrangement with the food bank, and provides pastoral support, but co-op members do all the rest. The result is a community of fifty former charity households who now "own" their own food cooperative, make and enforce their own rules, and support one another in countless ways. The idea has been so successful that the church has started five such co-ops and is replicating the model in several other cities. Accountability among members reinforces trust. And their integral relationship with the church is mutually respectful, honorable, and trustworthy.

What if we asked ourselves "What outcomes would we actually like to see from our charity?" and then began to restructure our giving to produce those very results. If we cared about, for instance, seeing human dignity enhanced, or trusting relationships being formed, or self-sufficiency increasing, then we could employ proven methods known to accomplish these goals. We know that trust grows with accountability over time. We know that mutual exchange and legitimate negotiating is energizing (people of every culture love to bargain!). And we know that employment starts people on the path to self-reliance. We know these things. And we have the capacity to accomplish them. But the will to change our traditional charity systems—now that is the real challenge.

## CHAPTER FIVE

## *Beyond Us-Based Giving*

EARLIER WE LOOKED AT HOW organizations and churches invest in religious tourism, often yielding the unintended consequence of turning service into pity and patronage. Behind this burgeoning movement is a technologically sophisticated marketing industry that employs innovations for promoting charitable engagement. These methods are used by churches and organizations across the country. Their approach is not always honest, and like cure-all elixirs peddled by snake-oil salesmen, many of the promises of mission-trip marketing do not measure up to the hype.

This chapter offers a deeper look at the compassion business, exploring who benefits from the industry and how self-interest influences even decisions made by worthy institutions.

Lately, I've been experiencing a new ecumenism. After losing my first wife Peggy to breast cancer, I have been blessed with a second Peggy who is a lifelong Catholic. Our Sunday worship alternates each week, one Sunday in the Catholic tradition, the next Sunday at my Presbyterian church. One similarity between the two churches is the common interest in mission trips. Last Sunday Father Mike ended the Mass with a plea for financial support for a mission trip to Mexico. He has already led several trips to Central American countries, experiences that "changed the lives of those who went." Fourteen people signed up for this Mexico trip, he announced, a good mix of teenagers and adults. But, Father Mike said, gently goading the congregation to participate, the Protestant churches are far out ahead of the Catholics in number of missioners. On his last trip to Nicaragua he observed several church groups, twenty to forty strong, clustered at the airports, wearing colorful T-shirts with catchy logos—all Protestants.

From within the folds of his flowing white vestment he pulled out a small plastic container, cylindrical in shape, about four inches long and the diameter of a quarter. "M&M's" he declared with a smile. "M&M's for everyone." My salivary glands reacted immediately. "**M**oney for **M**issions!" he declared buoyantly. The congregation would be given empty M&M containers to fill—quarters preferably, with bills and check fillers more than welcome. With everyone participating, he assured us, there would be more than enough money to cover the Mexico trip.

Creative idea, I thought, wondering where it originated.

When I got home, I Googled "mission trips" on my laptop. Popping up on my screen were numerous websites, sound and video enhanced, with captivating pictures and heart-touching words. "To love is to serve," Mission Discovery's tagline stated. Vying for the top Google spots were Real Impact Missions, Praying Pelican Missions, Blessing the Children, and Touching the World. Missions-Trip.com listed 379 approved mission-trip organizations covering nearly every country on the globe. Christianconnector.com offered a $1,000 missions scholarship drawing. MissionaryFundraiser.com won my emotional-appeal award: "From taking care of orphans in Swaziland, Africa, to ministering to natives in the Amazon jungles of Peru, we have all kinds of amazing locations available. You will come alive in your faith as you experience the thrill of serving and sacrificing for the sake of the Gospel. So what are you waiting for? Your mission field is waiting."

This is a lucrative growth industry run by entrepreneurs claiming they're "just wanting to serve the cause of Christ" even as they scramble for a market share. With somewhere between two and four million U.S. mission-trippers last year raising and spending billions of dollars, money is the grease that turns the spiritual wheels. And Father Mike obviously invested some of his budget on the M&M gimmick.

The Federal Trade Commission, an independent agency of the U.S. government, is charged with keeping American business free and fair. Included in its many responsibilities is the goal "to prevent the dissemination of false and deceptive advertising of goods, drugs, curative devices, and cosmetics." False claims, whether by large companies or car dealers, when detected, are subject to public exposure, penalties, and immediate corrective action. The FTC has jurisdiction over a broad spectrum of activities, but there is one realm it cannot penetrate—the church. The church-state barrier offers protection against government intrusion into the practice of organized religion. Of course, one would expect that, since the Judeo-Christian traditions are foundational to the ethical and moral codes of American society, the church would be the last institution in need of ethical policing.

Certainly the church is not without its flaws. The moral failure of church leaders is legendary. The media feeds off such scandal. Yet, in spite of the damage caused by the occasional fall of religious leaders, the church as an institution strives to preserve and protect high standards of conduct. Though its members, and too often its leaders, fail to measure up to its high ideals, the church remains the primary guardian of moral and ethical values. It may wrestle with controversial and divisive issues of the day, but it does so in pursuit of a moral high ground.

But there is one area that seems to have eluded the ethical scrutiny of the church—perhaps because the practice is so pervasive or because the claims seem so spiritual. Look at most any promotional package for a mission trip and you will get the distinct impression that lost, starving, forsaken people have their last hope riding on the willingness of U.S.

church groups to come and rescue them. The pictures are heartrending—a close-up of a child's sad face, a tin-roof shack beside an open sewage ditch, an old woman struggling under a load of firewood sticks. The emotional call goes out from Youthquests.com for "healed, trained, empowered, and Spirit filled teens to be missionaries to the world." Such experiences promise to touch lives, change the world, and have a dramatic, life-changing impact on those who will sacrifice their comfort to go. For a week!

Our "you can save them" rhetoric may be effective spin. Yes, there are Haiti earthquakes. But the overwhelming majority of our mission trips are to places where the needs are for development rather than emergency assistance. And development is about enabling indigenous people to help themselves. This requires a longer-term commitment, not the sort of involvement that lends itself to short-term mission trips.

Mission trips have value. They open up new worlds, new perspectives, new insights. They expose us to fascinating cultures, connect us with new friends, allow us to experience God at work in surprising ways, inspire us, break our hearts, build camaraderie among traveling companions. Any one of these benefits might well justify the time and expense. But isn't it time we admit to ourselves that mission trips are essentially for *our* benefit? Would it not be more forthright to call our junkets "insight trips" or "exchange programs"? Religious tourism would have much more integrity if we simply admitted that we're off to explore God's amazing work in the world.

The local church is an institution with institutional needs. It is important to understand this. It begins with an informal group of like-minded people who come together for fellowship and worship, it evolves into a structured organization with budgets and staff and buildings, and finally it matures into an enduring institution. It functions like all other institutions—with a stated mission and an intrinsic motivation to preserve and protect its own interests. The lion's share of church budgets are spent on meeting the needs of the congregation, not for the needs of outside communities. To earmark mission-trip expenditures as primarily for the spiritual benefit of members would be in keeping with traditional church budgeting. It is important to understand this so that we will not be disappointed by unrealistic expectations.

## The Toxic Mission Report

SPEAKING OF INSTITUTIONAL NEEDS, what serves the best interests of the church (or organization) does not necessarily benefit the people they intend to serve, as the following episodes illustrate.

*Missionary.* That's how I am listed on the annual missions report of a suburban church that supports our work in the city. My picture and monthly newsletter are placed on one of their main bulletin boards along with a score of other sponsored ministries and missionaries that serve all over the globe.

The church prays regularly for me. And each year I am invited to give a field report at their annual missions conference. For years this church body has been one of my most steady, dependable streams of income. They have played a significant role in enabling me to follow the call of God to serve among the poor, even as I have sought to be a faithful steward of their investment.

A while back I was invited to join their pastor and members of their missions committee for lunch at the church. For fellowship and encouragement, they said. Not far into the friendly chitchat, another agenda surfaced. They wanted to explore ways their church could be more personally involved in hands-on ministry in the city. Some of their members had volunteered with us, but that was some time ago, they reminded me. Now, the church wanted to reengage in service with us. In evaluating their missions giving, they wanted to strategically allocate funds, which meant having the personal participation of members in the ministries they supported.

It was a welcome offer. There are sports teams to coach, kids to tutor, houses to build, widows to visit. As I went down through a menu of opportunities, though, I could tell they were looking for something else. It eventually came out that they were looking for a monthly list of needs and service opportunities for church members to select from, and someone from our Focused Community Strategies staff to schedule and coordinate volunteer involvement.

It was a win-win approach, they assured me. Their missions dollars could both support their missionaries and at the same time allow them to be personally involved in missions. They might even consider upping my support level.

My mind went to the growing stack of demands that awaited me back at my office, each with immediate priority: the zoning hearing at city hall to determine if we could start construction on a house a family desperately needs, intrigue at the school-board meeting where a self-serving board member was attempting to torpedo our application for a new charter school, meeting with a banker who would give thumbs up or down on a property we had been working on for more than two years, and, always, the evictions, break-ins, arrests, run-aways, fights, all laced into the routine responsibilities of running an urban ministry.

My stomach tightened. Did these bright, efficiency-oriented, well-resourced church leaders think that I should drop frontline duties of organizing and managing the urban mission outreach to meet the needs of their congregation? And the not-so-subtle offer of a potential increase in financial support? That somehow felt more manipulative than supportive.

These were good people, friends, wanting to be faithful and intelligent leaders in their church. Time is money in their world. Return on investment (ROI) was responsible steward-ship. Getting a double return on their mission investment—support a missionary and support church volunteerism with the same dollar—this was good money management. Had

I been more desperate for their extra dollars, I might have agreed.

Instead, I encouraged them to create a position within the church—call it ministry of volunteer mobilization—that would take on this important mission. I would be delighted, I told them, to coordinate urban service opportunities with that person.

After that meeting, the church dropped my support.

More recently I have been in dialogue with another church, a rapidly growing young congregation in an upscale in-town area of Atlanta. They are a "seeker friendly" church attracting thousands of young professionals to media-rich services with live contemporary music and winsome gospel presentations. The leadership recognizes the importance of a "love God, love neighbor" theology and is encouraging their congregation to become actively engaged in service, especially among the less fortunate of the city. We have had a number of meetings to explore how their congregation might partner with our inner-city ministry.

The reservoir of talent in this church is daunting. Released into society, this energetic, highly skilled force could have amazingly redemptive impact. The church leaders recognize this awesome responsibility and are taking it very seriously. They have rejected the traditional church missions model (missions committee, budget, conference, and so forth) and have decided rather to put their energy behind mobilizing members to hands-on community service in a broad range of settings. Money follows vision, they have rightly concluded. The church's role is to raise their members' awareness to the needs, help connect them to opportunities, and let God do the rest. Last Saturday more than a hundred of these eager young professionals converged on our neighborhood to repair a widow's home, landscape a blind woman's yard, paint a community thrift store, pick up truckloads of trash and old tires, and engage in at least a dozen other community-enhancing tasks. The whole event cost our ministry nearly $4,000.

The church has made a decision not to give money to ministries like ours. On occasion they might offer a small donation to assist with a project their members participate in. But the real benefit, they told me, is the labor they provide.

This "real benefit" almost always costs our ministry money.

Better to leave funding decisions to the personal discretion of individual members, they tell us. For FCS, however, it becomes a real challenge to jump through a church's special hoops in the name of serving local communities and then raise funds from other sources in order to support the service projects of an affluent church.

This "tale of two churches" tees up this question: when a church makes decisions about serving others, are the ones being served the urban poor or the church?

I understand how good people wanting to do a good job end up creating self-serving systems. And how good churches led by busy people can devise ways to efficiently expedite their duties at the expense of others. But at some point, someone needs to raise the question, Is the church enabling missionaries to minister, or are the missionaries serving the needs of the church? Is the church lightening the load of the frontline workers, or are the troops on the ground bearing the weight of the church's efficiently run service projects?

## A Balanced Portfolio

How churches allocate their resources reveals their emphasis. How they manage their money reflects upon their stewardship. Should they follow sound investment counsel as advised by professional financial planners? My financial advisor tells me I should maintain a balanced portfolio, even in turbulent economic times. He says some of my retirement portfolio should be in stocks, some in bonds, some still in real estate, some in venture capital, some in international investments, some liquid in a money market—spread carefully across a range of investments that will yield optimal earnings over time with a conservative level of risk. He insists I diversify.

What if churches applied that same philosophy to the church investments, missions, and benevolence budgets. What would spreading our missions and outreach dollars across a broad range of local and foreign investments actually yield?

Missionaries, knowing the way churches allocate missions dollars, make the rounds to an ever-widening network of churches to secure modest financial commitments for their causes. It's a balanced portfolio approach that seems to work for both the church and the supported ministries. On the surface, at least.

When I sit down with my financial advisor to review my retirement account, he shows me how my investments are doing. The numbers tell the story. Real estate is down, some minor adjustments need to be made, stay with the long view, the yield will improve with the economy. But how do we measure the yield on service investments? The size of the budget doesn't tell us anything about impact. And the number of church members volunteering in outreach programs measures only *activity*, not *outcomes*.

If we are serious about significant impact, the missions we invest in must produce measurable results. And to achieve measurable change in the lives of the poor and the communities they inhabit, focused, not diversified, investment is required.

If we want to see substantial change in a troubled neighborhood, we must concentrate energies and resources there over time. It's a case that must be justified to foundations and other funding sources, since they understandably want to serve as many worthy causes as possible (as well as avoid the appearance of favoritism). Yet, the case must be made that disproportionate concentration of money, time, and effort is required to achieve significant and lasting change. Spreading investments thinly will yield only surface results, and temporary ones at that.

That's why our organization, Focused Community Strategies, works in only one neighborhood at a time. A simultaneous advance on all facets of community life—safety, education, housing, youth, seniors, church, block-by-block organizing, business—produces measurable results. The effort must be sustained over time to produce deep and permanent change. And this is costly. However, as neighborhood health improves, as economic forces take hold, as the fabric of the community is strengthened, the need for outside resources will diminish. This may take up to a decade.

Is it the same for church mission strategy? If a church were to examine its strengths—its culture—and identify the preponderance of professions of its members (educators? real estate agents? lawyers? accountants?), it might well discover the arena of service it is best capable of addressing—as well as its innate passions. A church full of businesspeople might be uniquely equipped to create successful businesses in a developing country. A church full of educators could turn around an underperforming school in their community, even the entire system.

By narrowing the focus of missions, by concentrating the collective efforts of the church on specific places and issues, we dramatically increase the chances of effecting significant, measurable, and lasting change.

Our congregations are full of compassionate, creative people with all manner of worthy causes that are close to their hearts. And I understand the desire (the need) of a pastor to keep his or her flock pacified (if not engaged). Thus the rationale for a broad, balanced mission portfolio. But I also know that all of us respond to inspired and intelligent leadership.

When the vision is right, people rise to a worthy challenge. When the leadership is committed to *outcomes* rather than *activity*, to measurable results rather than budget size or number of engaged members, changes in mission focus can be navigated with an acceptable level of disruption.

Maybe it's time to ditch the balanced portfolio and focus on outcomes.

Institutional self-interest is not confined to the church. All institutions—religious or secular, for-profit or nonprofit, public or private—feed it. Currently one highly respected international charity—the Salvation Army—is impaled on the horns of a self-interest dilemma. The largest grant ever offered to them may prove to compromise their historic mission.

### Toxic Hamburgers

ONE AND A HALF billion (that's a *b*) dollars is a pretty nice donation for any nonprofit to receive, let alone a Christian organization that works with the poor. That's exactly the windfall that came to the Salvation Army when Joan Kroc, heir of Ray Kroc's McDonald's hamburger fortune, died in 2003.

The Ray and Joan Kroc Center in San Diego had become one of Joan's favorite charitable projects after her husband's death. This magnificent 12.4-acre complex features an aquatic center complete with water-therapy services; a 56,000-square-foot fully equipped gymnasium; the only ice arena in southern San Diego County; a 30-foot-tall rock-climbing wall; a 33,000-square-foot performing arts center that houses a 600-seat theatre with a motorized orchestra pit, dance studio, and orchestra room; an education center; and office space for the Salvation Army. To fund this project, Joan donated $87 million of the fortune she had inherited from her late billionaire husband to the Salvation Army; $47 million of this gift was designated to build and equip this center, while the other $40 million was placed into an endowment to help subsidize its operating budget. There was nothing else like it in the world. Little wonder that she would view this as a model of community service worthy of the Kroc legacy. Her will directed executors to replicate Kroc Centers around the country.

And what better partner to implement her wishes than the Salvation Army? A 150-year history of serving the poor in 120 countries around the globe, this well-respected organization has remained faithful to the original mission launched by William and Catherine Booth in inner-city London in 1865. The Salvation Army "performs evangelical, social and charitable work and brings the Christian message to the poor, destitute and hungry by meeting both their physical and spiritual needs. Its ministry extends to all, regardless of ages, gender, color or creed." What an enormous affirmation for an organization to be granted $1.5 billion to establish state-of-the-art social service centers throughout the nation to further its mission while honoring the Kroc legacy!

For the past several years, the Salvation Army has been

busy establishing large, multipurpose social-service complexes in U.S. cities. The concept behind the centers is a holistic one—social, spiritual, mental, physical. It's a collaborative strategy that pulls together under one roof an array of serving agencies, both public and private, to produce a network of support for people in need. With cooperation and coordination among human-services providers, the quality and efficiency of service improve.

Or so the theory goes. At first glance, a new multi-million-dollar facility in a marginal area of town would seem to be a huge blessing. Recreation for the kids, accessible social workers, affordable day care for working moms—help for those treading hard to keep their noses above water. But what may be of benefit to some of the local residents may not be so favorable for their neighborhood at large. A concentration of programs in a large facility requires a large concentration of participants for those programs. This means drawing in clients from surrounding areas. The issue is not merely traffic and congestion. The real issue is the concentration of a needy and troubled population converging on a single neighborhood. Such an overconcentration of human need is unhealthy for any community, let alone one that is already struggling with its own share of challenges.

The large human-services institutional model (such as hospitals, treatment centers, churches, and so forth) increasingly finds itself at cross-purposes with the surrounding community. Many urban neighborhoods, after a half century of blight, are springing back to life as young professionals migrate back to the city. Gentrification is a new national norm that is reversing urban decline and restoring vitality to long-neglected areas. These new homeowners, along with many long-time residents, are understandably distressed to see institutions buying up residential properties to create parking decks and other equally imposing structures. It's called "institutional encroachment" upon a residential neighborhood. Local opposition arises not only because of the permanent loss of residential space but also from the traffic—both vehicular and human—that compromises the quality of community life. The large institutional model is essentially community unfriendly. A quick web search of current and recent lawsuits between neighborhood groups and institutions reveals the bitter animosity that institutional incursion stirs up.

Small is beautiful. At least in neighborhoods. The Salvation Army had it right when they established ministry centers that fit the scale of the neighborhoods they served. It has been their history for 150 years. But now, at the very time when our society is rediscovering the value of pedestrian-oriented, family-friendly communities, at this moment in our history when a younger generation is attempting to reweave the fabric of our tattered urban communities, this respected organization has been lured off course by a megagrant that is out of sync with the changing urban landscape.

Large institutions such as regional hospitals and shopping malls and megachurches do have their place. They fill an important role in our society. But they need space, lots of space, with acres of parking or multilevel parking decks and wide roads to accommodate the traffic. They work best in the spacious suburbs along expressways and in commercially zoned in-town areas designed to handle business traffic.

Admittedly, bigger is better when it comes to economies of scale—costs go down when you deal in bulk. There are efficiencies to gain. But there are also trade-offs. Like the drug-treatment organization we approached about establishing a center in our drug-ridden neighborhood. The group was interested in expanding their presence to the south side of town. The need was great and developable land was cheap and available. But when they came back with a plan for a thirty-bed facility complete with group-counseling rooms, commercial cafeteria, administrative offices, and ample parking lot, we put on the brakes. A quality drug-treatment program was certainly needed in our community, but an institutional facility dominating an entire residential block was hardly what we had in mind. Our desire was for a small-scale home or two (or a converted storefront) that would accommodate local needs, not import addicted people from all over the south side of the city. But the smaller-scale idea would not be feasible, we were told. It had to be of sufficient size in order for the numbers to work. In the best interests of the community we declined their offer.

Everything depends upon the lens through which we view reality. An institutional lens focuses on efficiency, accessibility, client-hours, cash flow, market share (i.e., a thriving business).

A community lens visions curb appeal, mothers pushing strollers, appreciating property values, safe parks, good schools, local businesses (i.e., a thriving community). Both views of reality are legitimate though seldom compatible. Each flourishes in different space. But because institutions (business, government, social, or religious) are often powered by big dollars, more often than not the community is backed into a defensive posture. And it is difficult to protest a project of high intentions like a church or hospital or Kroc Center. After all, what respectable, civic-minded person would oppose services to help his fellow human beings? The NIMBY (not in my backyard) reaction may be understandable, but it is hardly noble. It takes courage to stand up publicly against an institution whose mission is compassionate, especially when the community position sounds so self-serving. *Unless*, and this is a big unless, the community-development vision includes a healthy mix of smaller institutions that complement community growth. A health clinic rather than a sprawling hospital, a neighborhood church rather than a parking-hungry commuter church, a midsize grocery store rather than a shopping mall.

The Salvation Army had it right from the time it first deployed its dedicated troops throughout Dickens's London. They transformed putrid slums into healthy environments, one tenement, one block, one neighborhood at a time. Strange twist of fate, isn't it, that a ministry that has fed countless millions of poor slum-dwellers could be lured away from its historic mission by a hamburger?

# CHAPTER SIX

## *No Quick Fixes*

POVERTY IS A PLAGUE THAT infects nearly every nation on earth. Developed and underdeveloped countries alike struggle to overcome its debilitating effects. Whether Kinshasa or Kansas City, hunger and homelessness are pressing concerns—if different in severity. Big problems call for big solutions. Governments must get involved. Big corporations and big names can have a major impact. But in the same way that politics is local, so in the final analysis, all charity begins at home.

Top-down charity seldom works. Governments can give millions, rock bands can do benefit concerts, ex-presidents can champion causes, and churches can mobilize their volunteers. But in the end what takes place in the community, on the street, in the home, is what will ultimately determine the sustainability of any development.

In this chapter we look at the effectiveness (and often ineffectiveness) of inspiring ideas developed to combat poverty and the challenges faced in connecting these ideas at the grass roots for sustainable change.

## *Top-Down Charity*

ONE NIGHT WITHIN SIGHT of the Carter Center where Jimmy Carter houses his presidential library, office, and Atlanta apartment, a homeless man froze to death. The report in the morning news disturbed the former president. He had been all over the world taking on humanitarian causes—eliminating the dreaded guinea worm in Nigeria, overseeing democratic elections in developing countries, tripling grain output of peasant farmers in Africa. But here, right in his own backyard, people were dying from lack of adequate clothing and shelter. Sensitive to the needs of suffering humanity, he was compelled to do something to help. His cadre of researchers would soon report back to him their findings that Atlanta at that time (1990) was the poorest major city in the United States—more families living below the per-capita poverty line than in any other metropolitan area.

When you are an ex-president of the United States, a Noble Peace Prize winner, and a world-renowned humanitarian, you have at your beck and call an incredible number of powerful people and vast resources. To eliminate poverty in one city did not seem to President Carter an unreasonable challenge. Besides, Atlanta would be the host of the 1996 Olympic Summer Games, making it one of the most visible cities in modern history. National corporations and major foundations as well as a host of vested Atlanta interests would want to identify themselves with such a worthy effort. The timing was obviously right for a major assault on Atlanta poverty. So in 1991 Carter assembled some of his most trusted advisors and brightest minds and launched the Atlanta Project (TAP), the largest private antipoverty initiative in Atlanta and the boldest effort of its kind in the country.

The mission of TAP was to identify and eliminate Atlanta's deepest poverty. The strategy would focus the energies of corporate, government, religious, educational, social-service, and philanthropic sectors on twenty of the poorest communities in the city. Together with the residents, these resourced partners would chart a course to lead these communities out of poverty into economic, social, and spiritual health. It was a daunting undertaking, one so complex that only a president who had held the reins of the largest government in the world would attempt. But it was the right thing to do. And President Jimmy Carter was the right man for the job.

Carter's instincts were right. Everyone wanted to join him in this noble cause. A blue-ribbon cabinet was formed, a highly competent staff was recruited, a state-of-the-art communication center was established in the long-abandoned Sears warehouse. Corporations loaned executives and donated their wares, foundations poured in millions. In a remarkably short period of time, TAP was up and running, identifying community leadership and organizing grass-roots coalitions to facilitate the partnerships that would transform twenty inner-city neighborhoods.

Creating the organizational structure and support systems capable of coordinating the effort, though incredibly complex, proved to be the easy part. Building consensus among turf-guarding community leaders around a priority-needs list for their respective neighborhoods would be a far greater challenge. The twenty selected "communities" were in fact not communities at all. They were catchment districts defined by public schools, each comprised of several different neighborhoods with distinct histories, identities, and leadership. Viewed from the top, organizing community action through the public schools appeared to be the most logical strategy. From the grass-roots level, however, the picture was more complicated.

Had the goal been to provide more programs and better services for the poor, a top-down approach would have been reasonably easy to implement. Raise funds, hire more educators and social-service professionals, create job-training programs, expand Head Start—the kinds of poverty programs that the government was well experienced in running. But 1991 was a different time. Research was beginning to expose the ineffectiveness of four decades of this approach, and public opinion was shifting away from dependency-producing services toward more empowering models.

Jimmy Carter was committed to being on the cutting edge of social change. Community development was the wave of the future, his advisors counseled him. Urban neighborhoods needed empowering partners, not more publicly funded service providers. The mission of TAP was redefined—"to help urban communities gain access to the resources they need to solve the problems that most concern them."

But in 1991 few prominent professionals had any practical experience in bottom-up community transformation. Carter's cadre of experts knew at least theoretically the value of community empowerment and had adopted a community-development vocabulary. But most of the expertise in effective community work was in the domain of lesser-known practitioners who had yet to share their research in books. Had the president's council of strategists included an experienced community developer, the decision to target twenty multi-neighborhood school catchment districts would have been immediately challenged. A community developer would have known about the importance of neighborhood identity, how turf is jealously guarded by indigenous leaders, how long it takes outsiders to establish trust, how painstaking the process is of building consensus around neighborhood priorities. A community developer would have known instinctively that to create a new, unified "community" comprised of multiple, competing neighborhoods would be nearly impossible, even for an ex-president.

Within a year, a dizzying array of initiatives was ignited to impact the twenty distressed communities, each cluster containing approximately twenty-five thousand of the city's neediest residents. Partnerships were coordinated among schools, community groups, service agencies, government, and corporate leadership. World-class task forces were assembled to address juvenile violence, homelessness, unemployment, education. Atlanta's primary newspaper—the *Atlanta Journal & Constitution*—launched a new weekly section called City Life and devoted two full pages each week to TAP. "We are a part of the developing history of this city," stated program administrator Dr. Jane Smith.

Universities, international corporations, and government experts all offered support. Like an industrial-strength vacuum, TAP sucked in disproportionate amounts of philanthropic dollars. Everyone wanted in on the act. Volunteers flooded in by the thousands, and the full-time staff ballooned to eighty-nine.

Two and a half years into the project, however, the tangible results of all this activity were elusive. As reflected in TAP's annual report (bostonreview.net/BR19.3/barbash.html), the accomplishments were difficult to quantify.

Halfway through its initial five-year funding period, The Atlanta Project is not easy to evaluate. Lots of new relationships have been established, dozens of new initiatives are showing promise, more grant money is flowing into neighborhood revitalization, volunteerism is up, public awareness has been raised. But quantifying the impact of this effervescence—much less the credit TAP deserves for it—is impossible. Certainly, the basic indices of poverty in a population of more than half a million people are not likely to have improved in the 18 months since TAP became fully operational.

By year five, TAP was running out of gas. As Carter biographer Douglas Brinkley admits: "Everyone wants to volunteer for an event when a former president is there, whether it's building a house or knocking on doors. The initial enthusiasm that President Carter brought to the Atlanta Project couldn't be sustained." The lofty goals of eliminating poverty from the city had to be substantially downgraded. A far more humble admission appears in their reporting:

Like many comprehensive initiatives, TAP's complexity and scope remain difficult to evaluate because it is both an initiative and a collection of initiatives involving multiple sites, levels, and foci. TAP has learned a great deal since its inception. TAP doesn't claim to have all the answers, or the solution for eliminating urban decay. It hasn't solved the problem of unemployment; but it is working to create conditions that are ripe for economic development, entrepreneurship, and job creation. It hasn't solved the problems of juvenile violence, but it is looking at ways of getting youth involved in constructive and productive programs. TAP hasn't solved the homeless problem, but it is working with housing providers to keep some residents in structurally sound, clean, safe, and affordable housing. What TAP has done is come to understand that community involvement is a critical component in achieving true empowerment. The community must be empowered to act, initiate, make decisions and respond.

By 1997 the original twenty clusters were down to four consolidated offices "strategically located to serve a number of neighborhoods." According to an article on the Hoover Institute of Stanford University website, "Atlanta's Other Olympians," an internal audit criticized TAP for cultivating little input from the communities it serves, imposing cookie-cutter solutions from a bureaucratic central office, and focusing too much of its resources on small feel-good events like community cleanups. In a major restructuring effort, all of its eighty-nine full-time positions were eliminated. According to a cutting Stanford University analysis, "TAP's greatest achievement to date: consolidating application forms for social services from sixty-four pages to eight. All of this for $33.6 million."

Eight years after its inception TAP was bequeathed (along with a substantial grant from the Carter Center) to Georgia State University and disappeared into an expansive institutional bureaucracy. Its name was changed to Neighborhood

Collaborative, so as not to be confused with the already-existing Tuition Assistance Program. And its programmatic identity gradually shifted toward senior-citizen issues.

What lessons can we learn from President Carter's disappointing mission? The writer of Stanford's Hoover Institution article captured it well:

> If TAP typifies the flashy, top-down approach to community renewal, what follow are stories about the squads of private agencies engaged in a bareknuckled bout with poverty, homelessness, and crime. Unlike many nonprofits serving America's cities, these are not publicly funded extensions of government agencies. Nor do they receive the fanfare of an Olympic event. A tour of some of these ragtag, innovative organizations, each the product of dedicated citizenship, reveals what works in easing urban pathologies—one person, one family, one neighborhood at a time.

Given all the intelligence at his disposal, an ex-president should have known better than to operate on the erroneous assumption that top-down charity alleviates poverty and develops communities. But ex-presidents and other world leaders continue to toxify the very communities and countries they set about developing, especially when their priority is one-way aid.

## Dead Aid

DEAD AID—THIS IS WHAT Zambian-born economist Dambisa Moyo, in her book of the same title, calls the $1 trillion in charitable aid that has flowed into Africa over the past fifty years. Intended to save lives, to cure diseases, bolster struggling economies, and stimulate productivity, these streams of charity flowing in from prosperous nations around the globe have produced the opposite effects. Productivity has declined, corruption has increased, survival stress perpetually erupts in violence, millions have died. Why, asks Moyo, do the majority of countries of her continent "flounder in a seemingly never-ending cycle of corruption, disease, poverty, and aid-dependency" despite the fact that sub-Saharan countries have received more than $300 billion in development assistance since 1970?

Emergency, charity-based, and government—are the three forms of aid flowing into Africa. Aid from foreign governments in the form of loans (seldom repaid) and outright grants form by far the largest of these tributaries. Many fight for control over the allocation of these billions. And corruption, nepotism, and political intrigue festers around the mouths of these streams. The ensuing feeding frenzies gorge on resources intended to benefit the poor. Zaire's President Mobutu Sese Seko, for example, is estimated to have personally skimmed $5 billion—an amount equivalent to the entire external debt of his country. Not only does aid foment political instability and corruption, it discourages free enterprise—like the African mosquito-netting manufacturer who was put out of business by well-meaning charities that handed out millions of free nets.

At every level of African society the impacts of aid can be felt. Are African people better off for the $1 trillion that has poured in over the past half century from benevolent donors? "No," says Moyo. "In fact, across the globe the recipients of this aid are worse off; much worse off." It is a myth, Moyo says, that aid can eliminate systemic poverty. After years of personal observation and careful research, Moyo has concluded: "Aid has been, and continues to be, an unmitigated political, economic, and humanitarian disaster for most parts of the developing world."

So why is humanitarian aid still so popular? Why does it continue to be a moral imperative among the affluent cultures to impose charity on the less fortunate? Why do the Oprahs and Bonos, the USAIDs and Millennium Challenge Corporations, the national churches and parachurch agencies, the local church service-project volunteers and mission-trippers all buy into the belief that giving to the poor is a good thing?

The heart! That's what moves us to help. It's that imprint of the divine, the essential attribute of our humanness, that impels us to reach out, even sacrificially, to help another in distress.

Because our spiritual instincts feel so righteous, we are tempted to organize them into causes and cultural commodities: a hungry child becomes a Save the Children organization. Once institutionalized, these causes become commodities to market, fund, replicate. Helping a needy family repair their home becomes a ratings-hungry *Extreme Makeover: Home Edition* reality TV show. Programmed charity may not necessarily be a negative. However, it often focuses its energies on program advancement, using anecdotal results to promote its interests, while neglecting examination of the longer-term outcomes. As long as there are heartwarming stories to tell, well-marketed efforts can flourish for years—decades—without scrutiny. Africa bears this out.

"After more than five decades of the wrong diagnosis, it is time now to turn the corner and take the hard but indisputably better road. It is the clarion call for change." Since as an economist, Moyo's "better road" is understandably economic in orientation, she urges aid recipients to do the following:

- Get off aid.
- Promote entrepreneurship.
- Promote free trade.
- Invest in infrastructure.
- Secure reasonable loans, not grants.
- Encourage stable homeownership.

Though she aims primarily at government policies, her message is unmistakably clear to the nongovernmental organization (NGO) and religious sectors as well.

- Don't subsidize poverty.

- Reinforce productive work.

- Create producers, not beggars.

- Invest in self-sufficiency.

It's economists like Moyo who understand the riptide of toxic aid and take the risk of saying "No more!" Other bright visionaries stimulated by compassionate impulses seek to rise to the challenge, developing comprehensive, coordinated systems. I met with one such visionary with an exciting strategy for creating the first hunger-free city in America. His innovative plan, however, though impressive, omitted one important element.

## *Hurry Is the Enemy of Effectiveness*

THE BRAINCHILD OF A sharp entrepreneurial-type Christian businessman with a concern for the poor and a mind that thrives on solving big problems, the idea was brilliant: make Kansas City the first hunger-free zone in the country. We sat in the pastor's office of a prominent Baptist church, a church that had taken the lead in convening the city's decision makers around the issues of poverty. This was far more than a mere feed-the-hungry program—it was a community-building initiative to mobilize people of faith and goodwill to join together in a visible expression of compassion in their own neighborhoods. It would serve to unite churches across denominational barriers as they reached out to serve others in need.

Perhaps this would become a model for other cities plagued by similar issues of hunger. The problem was clearly reaching epidemic proportions:

- One in six Americans faces hunger during any given year.
- Over fifty million Americans are considered "food insecure."
- 5.7 million households per week receive emergency food.
- Seventeen million children and six million seniors face the threat of hunger.
- Between 2006 and 2008, the United States saw a 115 percent increase in hunger, and into 2011, it is continuously rising.

With the urgency of the issue driving him, the man with the plan leaned forward as he explained how the strategy would abolish hunger in his city. The technology and data are already in place, he said, that identifies every church member in the greater Kansas City area—names, ages, where they live, phone numbers, email addresses, employment status, church membership. This information can be assembled and printed on plat maps of every neighborhood in the city, block by block, house by house. The maps will be distributed to all the churches so everyone in a church can know where other Christians in their community are located. With their churches' blessing and encouragement, church members would contact other church members who live on their block, get acquainted, or-ganize food collections from their neighbors and take the food to various collection points for distribution to the needy. As churches get behind the effort—organize their parishioners, post the number of membership groups being formed, report the quantity of food being gathered—momentum will build and a contagion of compassion will spread across the city. Based on reliable estimates of the number of residents at or below the poverty line, the quantity of food that could be col-lected each month is, in conservative estimates, far in excess of the need.

"How do you keep your data current?" I inquired. With so much mobility in our society, so many people moving, chang-ing jobs and churches, data would be outdated within a year or two. "You don't want to know," the entrepreneur smiled. Corporations with highly secured computers gather, store, organize, and report everything about us, from our favorite cereals to the kinds of cars we drive. "The data is available," he assured me, "for a price."

"And how do you get churches to cooperate?" I asked. I know something about denominational competition, even between churches of the same stripe. His answer intrigued me. The food gathering would not be in the name of any particular church. It would be neighbors cooperating together around a cause that has broad appeal. Who would not want to eliminate hunger? It would attract not just church-goers but compassionate people from every sector, promoting a sense of community, a common need that neighbors recognize.

I fired one question after another—funding, staffing, scale, collection points, warehousing, transportation. Every question got a reasoned response. The plan had massive logistical and coordinating challenges, but the costs were modest, and both human and physical resources were available for mobilizing. In less than an hour of intense discussion I had become almost persuaded that Kansas City might well become the first hunger-free city in the country.

But one question remained: distribution. How would tons of collected food actually reach hungry stomachs? Who would ensure proper distribution? Would this food be given away? By whom, in what quantities, under what circumstances? And for a free-food program, what safeguards would prevent multiple dipping, hoarding, reselling food for drugs? What would keep this program from fostering unhealthy dependency and becoming another entitlement program? Utilizing the existing distribution mechanisms in the city—church food pantries, homeless shelters, feeding stations—did not adequately address these troubling questions.

"We need to get the program going, and soon," the entrepreneur said, returning to his sell. "Charlotte, North Carolina, has picked up on the idea, and we want to be first in the nation to roll it out!" I understood his urgency. Without the distinction of being first, Kansas City would lose marketing spark. Besides, Kansas City was ready now with a vetted plan, a set of churches responding favorably, and support from city government and the social-service community. Now was the time to declare Kansas City the first hunger-free city in the United States.

The distribution problem could be fixed on the way, he said, convincing himself. But doubling, even tripling, distribution outlets in the city would not address the dependency problem. Computer programs might reduce abuse of the system, but they would still separate people as "donor" or "recipient." Computers could not reconcile alienated relationships nor restore damaged dignity.

A massive and sustained food drive says much about the compassion of a city, and I admire the Kansas City spirit. The hard part, however, does not lie in the creation of new models—food-buying co-ops, food for community service, wholesale outlets. The hard part is rethinking the entrenched giveaway mentality and restructuring an established one-way charity system. A hunger-free zone may be possible, but developing the dependency-free zone is the real challenge.

For disadvantaged people to flourish into their full, God-given potential, they must leave behind dependencies that impede their growth. Initiatives that thwart their development, though rightly motivated, must be restructured to reinforce self-sufficiency if they are to become agents of lasting and positive change.

# CHAPTER SEVEN

# *Wise Giving*

IT MADE HUGE HEADLINES WHEN two of the world's richest people announced they were giving away their billions. Like the Rockefellers and Carnegies of an earlier generation, Warren Buffett and Bill Gates have made a joint commitment to give away the lion's share of their vast wealth to take on global challenges of gigantic proportions—like ending nuclear proliferation and curing AIDS. And they are inviting other members of this elite billionaires club to join them. Philanthropy at the rarefied levels of society is gaining in popularity. We can learn from how they are going about giving away their money. In this chapter we will meet some who are leaders in thinking through their giving strategies.

In a recent highly exclusive gathering of the world's wealthiest businesspeople, Buffett and Gates explained their rationale for giving back. They and their families had all that they would ever need, and so they concluded that the surplus should be reinvested to make the world a better place for humanity. When they opened the floor for discussion, two questions immediately surfaced: how do you give wisely, and how much should you give to your children?

"It's much easier to make [money] than it is to give it away *intelligently* (emphasis mine)," Buffett admitted in an interview with Christiane Amanpour on ABC News. Anyone can give money away indiscriminately. Successful entrepreneurs, however, are concerned with return on investment. They want to see measurable impact and lasting results. They are willing to take risks—risk-reward ratios are their stock-in-trade. But softhearted charity that doesn't offer permanent solutions lacks appeal for them. They want to eradicate a disease, save a failing educational system, find a new ecofriendly energy source.

Buffett was joined by Bill and Melinda Gates on the CNN show, where they offered their personal philosophies on responsible giving:

- R&D is vital.

- Invest in success: sound business principles also are good principles for responsible charitable investing.

- Focus on your passions.

- Investigate the best practices of those in the field to determine what works.

- Create a prototype to test new approaches.

- Record the process.

- Document the findings.

- Tweak the methods.

- Replicate successes.

If this new generation of philanthropists is to be as successful in their charitable endeavors as in their business careers, they will apply these same standards of due diligence.

Melinda Gates has a passion to fix the failing public education system in the United States, a system that has dropped from first to twelfth among industrialized nations in preparing college-ready graduates. She and her team have invested significant amounts of time, energy, and resources analyzing the problem. They have spent countless hours listening to students, parents, educators, and administrators; researching instructional methods, incentives, and organizational models; scrutinizing demographic influences; and studying models with promise.

In measured ways the Gates are funding innovative projects aimed at finding the most effective ways to enhance educational quality. In one school in Appalachia, for example, they have funded the installation of video cameras in classrooms so that teachers can study the full scope of activity within their learning environments and critique their own classroom management. Like football coaches reviewing with their players the films of the previous game, teachers are able to replay the full range of classroom dynamics—teaching techniques that connect, effective reinforcements, fatigue levels, missed opportunities, distractions, and ineffective responses.

Like these billionaires, we also can conduct a detailed assessment of our current benevolence portfolio:

- Is it yielding good returns?
- Is it consistent with our passions?
- Does it reflect our values about relief vs. development?
- Is it invested on the cutting edge?

Due diligence is the cornerstone of wise giving.

How do we calculate return on investment (ROI)? This can be tricky. Emergency assistance is easily measured by the number of victims served, the per-person cost being a discrete dollar number that can be compared to industry norms. Yet food pantry folk and disaster-relief organizations use the same language to describe their mission. Overhead percentage and cost per client, even though indicators of efficiency, are hardly the right measures of *effectiveness* when empowerment is the goal.

Buffett's wisdom? "Take the long view":

- Are recipients assuming greater levels of control over their own lives or do they show up, year after year, with their hands out?

- Is leadership emerging among the served?

- Are their aspirations on the rise?

- Is there a positive trajectory?

Though often difficult to quantify, such measures may prove better indicators of ROI than budget analyses and head counts.

In for-profit corporations on the cutting edge of their fields, research and development (R&D) is key. Yet seldom do nonprofits spend money on R&D, with universities and medical research being notable exceptions.

Innovation and risk taking are at least as important to the world of compassion as to the world of business. Organizations that test new methods and document their trial-and-error findings are likely to be the ones that shape the best practices of the future. Beware, however, of betterment programs that showcase state-of-the-art, computerized, fraud-proof systems. They still may be subsidizing indolence and fostering dependency. But this type of research combined with on-the-ground personal research is key, offering checks and balances.

With strong research in place, personal involvement offers the best way to determine if our charitable investments are being put to good use. Taking an insight trip, serving on a board, volunteering for a service project—these help us get a picture of the inside operations of a ministry. Personal acquaintance with the leader of an organization helps to validate its integrity. For the more entrepreneurial investor, innovation may be the most satisfying approach—launching a new venture with a skilled team to create a replicable prototype that could yield history-shaping solutions. The slickness of the marketing material is not always the best indicator of the soundness of the investment.

But R&D is not where transformational charity stops. Coming to the aid of a person (or village or nation) in need is what opens the door to a world of complex, interconnected challenges, and allows us to move fully into community involvement.

## Controlling the Lake

FEED A MAN A fish and he'll eat for a day; teach a man to fish and he'll eat for a lifetime. It's conventional wisdom.

But what happens when the fish disappear from the lake due to pollution or overfishing?

Then it's time for a change of strategy. Someone has to figure out how to get control of the lake: stop the pollutants, issue fishing licenses, put wildlife-management policies in place. Teaching a man to fish is an individual matter; but gaining control of the lake is a community issue.

That's why we call it "community development" and not human services. While those of us in community development value personal, hands-on, high-touch ministry, we also see that there are larger issues that have an impact on a person's potential for growth. What good is job training if the available jobs won't enable a man to support his family? Or what benefit is homeownership if the home is in a deteriorating, crime-infested neighborhood? If we are to teach people to both fish *and thrive*, we must figure out how to make use of the lake's potential.

Take the example of the yucca farmers of Nicaragua. When community developer Geralyn Sheehan asked a group of peasant farmers why they didn't grow more yucca on their idle land, they told her that they were growing all they could eat. When she asked why they didn't grow yucca to sell at the market, they explained that yucca begins to wither within three days, making it unmarketable. These men knew how to fish. But their isolation kept them from thriving.

Could community development principles tested in U.S. cities work in any poor rural environment? Focused Community Strategies, seasoned in Stateside urban development, was ready to expand its mission and join in a new challenge. Joint-venturing with Opportunity International, we embarked on a pilot study in Nicaragua—the poorest of the Central American countries. And Geralyn, our Minnesota-bred blonde-haired community developer and fluent Spanish speaker, moved in with the local peasants and began first to observe and to listen and then eventually ask questions. She also learned to enjoy the taste of yucca, called cassava, a sweet-potato-like staple of the Central American diet.

And she couldn't help but ask the obvious question: "Why don't you grow more of it?"

A good community developer is both curious and entre-preneurial. Geralyn was both. Her visits to the large produce market in Managua and conversations with local produce merchants and agronomists and exporters surfaced a wealth of important information about yucca: The yucca her neighbor farmers grew was utilitarian grade at best, adequate for family consumption but not the quality demanded by national and international markets. Export-grade yucca had to be treated with a preservative paraffin coating to give it a shelf life of forty-five to sixty days. She was pleased to learn that the soil in her mountain community was fertile, volcanic, and excellent for growing yucca, and that the rainfall was plentiful. There was potential there; Geralyn could see it. But in order to take full advantage of this opportunity, substantial changes would be required.

Hybrid starts of export-quality yucca were available in the country for a price. Paraffin processing equipment was tech-nologically simple and relatively inexpensive. The markets were accessible. But—and this was significant—at least forty farmers, each planting five acres of hybrid yucca, would be required to sustain the operation.

The profit potential was alluring—three times what their current crop would bring—but the risks, daunting. It meant letting go of a practice that had kept their families fed for gen-erations, taking out loans to buy plants they had never before grown, hiring an agronomist to consult with them on planting, fertilizing, processing, and marketing their harvest—all on a gamble that the bright ideas of an outsider could be trusted.

Twelve farmers took the gamble—not enough to sustain a processing plant but enough to test the theory that a harvest of hybrid yucca, rushed to a prearranged wholesaler at the central market, would yield a handsome return. With their own meager savings, loans from our microlending partner, and back-breaking labor with oxen and wooden plows, twelve peasant farmers took their first courageous steps into the unknown world of agribusiness.

Two and a half months later, twelve proud farmers gathered in a waist-high field of lush hybrid yucca, admiring together the early growth of their investments. It would be several months more before harvesttime, but the well-formed subsoil tubers were maturing nicely. And these were not the only admirers gathering that day. A delegation representing forty other farmers arrived, farmers who had passed up the initial offer, now eager to be included in the next.

Success breeds success. Now there would be economies of scale to sustain the paraffin operation. And that means value added to the crop, new packaging and trucking job opportunities, and marketing streams that could flow to regions as far away as Miami.

Those who understand transformational investment understand how peasant yucca farmers now dream dreams never before accessible to them. Perhaps they are the forerunners of a fertile growing region that will supply basic nutrition to the tables of millions of Central Americans. Perhaps their children will go to college and return to lead a burgeoning agricultural economy. The dreams of achievers know few bounds, even as, on the other hand, the aspirations of survivors seldom have opportunities to rise above subsistence living.

Controlling the lake implies ownership *by* the community *of* their community. This begins with a change of perspective. For those in Western urban communities it means that instead of viewing the neighborhood as a place the lucky escape from, workers must see that within their neighborhoods are resources that can be exploited for the benefit of residents. Sometimes it takes someone with a fresh, outside perspective to seed a vision of economic potential greater than the familiar, deadly economies of drugs and prostitution. And this person must ask the question, Who owns the land (the lake)?

- Who owns the crack house? How do we get control of it?

- Who owns the abandoned warehouse? How can we retrofit it for lofts?

- Who owns the vacant lot? How do we get the tires and trash cleared off it?

- Who owns the vacant storefront? Can it be reclaimed as a community restaurant?

Controlling the lake is a community affair, the domain of neighbors vested in reclaiming their turf. And it is grounded in the belief that assets are available to be harvested from a place others view only as wasteland. That belief must be strong enough to risk the investment of personal time, money, and energy.

How is such a community vision birthed? The reality is that the dreams are already there: longings for a better life for their children, hopes that their labor will someday produce a more prosperous future. But in isolated U.S. urban ghettos, or in isolated rural villages in Nicaragua, the dreamers are seldom connected to the resources that provide nutrients to give those dreams life—that is, until by chance or by providence, someone in the village meets a connected person with a heart, a person who has time to listen, a person with both imagination and resources. Hope, smothered dim under years of survival pressures, begins to flicker once again. In time, after the trustworthiness of the connecting person can be tested, after the opportunity is subjected to ample reality testing, hope can have free rein. It is a dangerous, fragile, exhilarating moment when the poor cast off their restraints and begin to believe. And this transformative moment, more than any other moment, is what the community developer lives for and what the community thirsts for.

## The Microlending Model

OPPORTUNITY INTERNATIONAL'S WORK LARGELY focuses on microlending as a model for assisting the poor in economic development. The organization makes many thousands of small loans to struggling peasants all over the globe. Its primary lending method is "trust groups," an innovative approach developed in Bangladesh by Nobel Peace Prize–winner Muhammad Yunus.

The very poor have no tangible assets to guarantee loans needed to grow their tiny microbusinesses—no homes, no cars, no livestock suitable as collateral. But one asset that many peasants do have—one that can be as valuable as physical assets—is community interdependence and trust. By promising to stand good for one another's loans, a group of twenty to thirty entrepreneurial women (95 percent are women) can offer a lender an acceptable level of security. These "trust groups" over time have demonstrated an amazingly high percentage of on-time loan repayment. Using this method, Opportunity International enables peasants in the poorest regions of the world to grow their subsistence enterprises—roadside fruit stands, bread baking, sewing—to produce greater volume and higher income for their families.

Atlanta businessman and FCS board member David Allman was invited to a fund-raising event sponsored by Opportunity International. After the presentation, David inquired if the organization ever engaged trust groups in specifically focused community-development activities. Twenty years of involvement with FCS had taught him that community development can increase the wealth and well-being of the whole village, not just individual entrepreneurs. A microloan may help a family buy a cart to haul their produce but it will not pave a road made impassible during the rainy season—that takes community development.

A generative discussion ensued that yielded some unexpected results. Opportunity International, which has entrepreneurial DNA in its blood, was intrigued by the idea of combining microfinance with community development to see if it added significant value to their lending model. A five-year joint venture pilot project was launched to test the concept. Nicaragua was selected for the test site, and a new Opportunity International–Nicaragua board was formed. David Allman became its chair. That's how Geralyn Sheehan was hired and deployed. Her work with the yucca farmers, among other projects, provided sources for studies and observations that continue to unfold like a blooming flower.

It took several months for Geralyn (and her teenage daughter) to acclimate to the Nicaraguan culture, settle into a town in a rural region, meet area trust-group members, and explore ways to begin introducing cooperative thinking. Her first initiative was to offer low-interest loans to any small group of neighbors (three or more) who had an idea to collectively expand their businesses. She called it the "idea fund." A number of locals applied. Several bread makers wanted to invest together in a large community oven that would increase their production capacity. Some fishermen wanted to invest in a community dock to enhance their fishing businesses as well as attract a new tourist market. Several parents wanted to establish a self-supporting lending library at their village school, which had no books.

And the twelve yucca farmers took out loans to plant the hybrid strain of the crop, yielding significantly higher profits on the national market.

These were not the only growth industries emerging through the collective efforts of villagers. Local artisans came together to form a co-op to promote their products. They created *Ojalá* (if God be willing), a brand name to give them an identity in the marketplace. Their co-op, named NicaWorks, employed dozens of artisans, sewers, potters, and wood-carvers, conducted market research, provided quality control, and connected these craftspeople to wholesale and retail markets both nationally and internationally.

Over these five years it has become apparent to Opportunity International that the economic impact of their microlending program could be increased exponentially by twinning it with community development. They have extended the five-year pilot for another five years to pursue additional opportunities in Nicaragua and to initiate a replication strategy in other countries.

Through the first of those five years of the study, Geralyn carefully documented her activities and outlined some significant insights. The following is adapted from curriculum she is developing to train Opportunity International staff and other service organizations to enhance their programs through community economic development. (Used by permission of

Geralyn Sheehan and Opportunity International.) She provides a wonderful model for the kind of due diligence needed to make sure we are wise givers.

What questions should we be asking ourselves about *community building* work?

- **Who are the producers?** *In community building, the producers must be members of the community. If outside actors are principally responsible for results, then the community will never change, be strengthened, or advance its capacity to deal with its own problems, solutions, and development.*

- **Where is the energy?** *Always follow the energy in the community. When initiating a project, don't worry about the scale or impact. Be concerned with the amount of energy and passion behind the project. When there's energy and passion, then you won't have a problem getting local people to take the lead.*

- **What's the "win" and is it achievable?** *Start where people are. If they have never worked together, then a first project may be humble but can be the right project for the community to have a "win." Many poor communities need to feel the joy of succeeding. This inspires future action and commitment. Success breeds success. And one organized project always leads to learning and* *the ability of the community to take on a larger project next time.*

- **Who are the principal investors?** *Multiple investors are ideal and* always *should include community members, local associations, and/or local institutions. Local residents that will benefit from the project should be approached as the "first" investors in a project. Expect some level of cash and, if needed, sweat equity as part of their contribution. (If they aren't willing to put their money in, then we don't want to put our money in.) Don't dismiss other resources that can come from community members such as organizing childcare, providing food for workers, lending carts, tools, horses, etc.*

- **What's the organizing mechanism?** *If your goal is to build community capacity, then there needs to be investment in a local community entity. This can take the form of an association, business, and/or cooperative. Invest resources in building capacity for organizing and maintaining community unity.*

What questions should we be asking ourselves about *community economic development* work?

- **What are the local assets of our clients?** *Begin with a database of client products, skills, abilities, and* *dreams. Focus on households, not just the loan client. Client's livelihoods are based on the household economic activity, not on the sole business receiving a loan. We need to see the world as our clients see their world. Build plans and opportunities from this perspective.*

- **What are the assets of this place?** *Assess local potential by capturing data on local associations, natural resources, physical assets, businesses, institutions, and local methods of exchange.*

- **What's happening in the local, national, and international markets?** *Once we know our client's products, skills, and interests and we know the local assets, we are now ready to review these assets in light of market opportunities. Using market data, research, and studies can assist in forming strategies that respond to local resources. This may uncover potential connections to grow businesses, enter markets, and assess what industries have the greatest potential for the poor.*

- **How are entrepreneurs supported?** *If we want to grow local economies, then we need to invest in both building the capacity of local entrepreneurs AND in a "feeder" system for growing future entrepreneurs. Creating mechanisms that support entrepreneurs should include peer-to-peer exchanges, financing, relationship building (which can lead to partnerships and opportunity identifi-*

*cation among businesses), and a respectful environment to confront entrepreneurs' business issues and tough realities. We also need to invest in training youth as future entrepreneurs. Preparing youth with an entrepreneurial perspective will assure that they are prepared to enter the job market as entrepreneurs, equipped to expand existing businesses or start their own new business successfully.*

## Does Microlending Work in the United States?

MICROLENDING HAS NOW GONE mainstream. Once the exclusive domain of nonprofits, this model has now been proven to be a legitimate and profitable means to get needed capital into the hands of struggling entrepreneurs—and now the international banking and investment industries have joined in. While it costs more to service small loans for people in remote areas than in large cities, repayment rates are generally good.

So why don't we do more microlending to the poor in the United States?

Experienced microlending organizations have identified three essential elements for successful microloans: The borrower must have (1) an ingrained work ethic, (2) a demonstrated entrepreneurial instinct, and (3) a stable support system. Like legs on a three-legged stool, all three must undergird the borrower or the transaction will not stand.

In developing countries where people must constantly hustle simply to survive, a *work ethic* is almost a given. Not so in a culture like the United States, where the welfare system has fostered generations of dependency and has severely eroded the work ethic. Where a people assume that their subsistence is guaranteed, hard work becomes neither a necessity for survival nor a means to escape poverty.

*Entrepreneurship* is also very common in developing cultures. Roadside fruit stands, firewood selling, craft making—these and a host of other small unregulated enterprises proliferate along rural roads and urban thoroughfares and are the primary sources of family income that often involve the work of an entire family. Additional capital to increase production and marketing capacities is a highly valued treasure that directly translates into an improved standard of living. But in poorer U.S. communities, legitimate businesses are much harder to operate. We have complex regulations that require proper zoning, business licensing, insurance coverages, accounting systems, IRS reporting; the list is daunting (and expensive) for the entrepreneur who has a dream of running his or her own business. In our highly competitive economy where roughly 85 percent of new businesses fail within the first two years, the survival odds for a sustainable inner-city business are even more daunting. More often than not, the would-be business owner resorts to informal, if not illegal, enterprises that operate under the radar and do not leave a paper trail, enterprises that microlending organizations understandably shy away from.

A stable *support system* is a survival mechanism in a developing culture. Families must pull together, children are an important part of the workforce, the elderly provide infant care, farmers combine efforts at harvest. In addition to family support, many microlenders establish trust groups of community residents who co-collateralize one another's loans, pledging their combined, often meager assets to guarantee the loans of participating members. This communal support provides both collateral and accountability. Everyone realizes that on-time loan repayments are essential to keep the life-giving capital flowing to the community.

In the United States the number of two-parent nuclear families is in decline. Among the urban poor they have become a rarity. With the family structure broken in a society that values individualism above collectivism, neither interdependent family support nor community support is reliable. The third leg of the microlending stool is virtually absent.

The one exception where microlending seems to work rather well in the United States is among first-generation immigrants from underdeveloped (though industrious) countries. Vietnamese from a fishing culture, for example, know innately how to catch and market seafood. Their families have survived on this activity for generations. With a microloan to purchase a small boat and fishing gear, an extended family will pull together, invest long hours of toil, and carve out a niche in the seafood industry. Where there remains intact the foundational pillars of work ethic, entrepreneurial instinct, and social support, the chances are quite likely that microlending will work well.

IT HAD BEEN TWO YEARS since aging peasant farmer Don Blas interrupted a "trust group" business meeting of village women with yet another plea for them to support his well project. Like scores of speeches before, this one fell on deaf ears. The women were far too busy negotiating tiny loans to increase the volume of tacos and fruit at their roadside stands—business that could generate immediate córdobas for their families. Don Blas's vision of fresh water flowing to every home in the village was being dismissed once again as an old man's fantasy. But at this gathering a different set of ears was listening. For the first time a community developer was sitting in their midst.

"What would it cost to do the well?" a new voice in the circle asked. All eyes cut to Geralyn, recently arrived in Nicaragua from the States. Don Blas did not know. He had over the years learned some rudimentary mechanics about wells. But, he admitted with some embarrassment, he did not know his numbers. The women *did* know their numbers, though, observed Geralyn. They worked with numbers every day, buying and selling produce, paying back loans, squirreling away precious savings. Would Don Blas and the village men be willing to join with the women to assemble a business plan for the well? Only someone from outside the culture would dare suggest such a thing. And would villagers risk their own meager resources as equity for a loan for the project?

Within a year, a deep well (mentioned in chapter 2) was supplying an ample water flow to two hundred households! The men dug trenches and laid water lines while the women prepared food and tended to the finances. A village water commission had been elected to set fees, collect monthly water bills, manage the budget, pay back the loan, and oversee maintenance. For the first time the village owned a wealth-generating asset that benefited every family, and—perhaps even more significant—they owned an enterprise that allowed their dreams to rise above mere survival.

During the next few months dreams began to flourish in that little Nicaraguan village of La Laguna. The water commission soon realized it needed an office for keeping records, collecting water bills, and scheduling meetings. The local public school had available space. The school also needed water. A deal was struck to provide office space in exchange for water for the school from the village well. And this was only the beginning.

The adjoining village had no water supply. La Laguna's well was producing more water than village households were using. Discussions began about selling water to the neighboring village.

With the well funding the dreams and goals of the community, the village leadership turned their attention toward a growing concern for the poorest families in the community whose homes needed serious repair. Leaking roofs was a major problem. During the rainy season water poured into their dirt-floor homes turning them into muddy, damp hovels. Clothes never dried. Children were never clean. In a recent meeting with Geralyn, Don Blas presented another proposal for a community loan to address this pressing health need. They would like to purchase a bulk supply of corrugated zinc roofing to resell to villagers to fix their roofs (at a small profit for the community). They had calculated, based on household incomes, that it would take two to three years to repay the loan.

"But what about the neediest families who could not afford a new roof, even if they had three years to repay?" The question had to be asked. "In phases" came the well-reasoned response. Sell them enough panels to cover one third of the wettest part of their house. When that is paid off, they can purchase a second installment of roofing, until the whole house is finally dry. It would take considerably more time to do it this way, but it would extend to everyone in the village the opportunity to improve their own lives at their own pace. Even the poorest could participate with dignity.

Investment in local development transformed this community. No more well-meaning churches and aid agencies "helping the poor." Don Blas and his La Laguna neighbors became a prophetic voice to Western nonprofit models: invest with communities as they invest to transform their own futures.

# CHAPTER EIGHT

## *Take the Oath*

IN CHAPTER 1 WE LOOKED briefly at the Oath for Compassionate Service. Its well-known precursor in the medical field—the Hippocratic Oath—concludes with this principle: *Above all, do no harm.* Hippocrates (460–377 BC), the Father of Modern Medicine, recognized the power of the healing profession to effect great good as well as potentially do harm. The oath that he instituted, a pledge taken by doctors to this day, established ethical standards for physicians' conduct, which included patient confidentiality, referral for specialized treatment, sharing of medical knowledge, and valuing prevention above cure. The Hippocratic Oath requires that physicians be personal and caring, put the interests of patients first in medical decisions, strive always to preserve life, and never play God by taking life.

In that same spirit the following oath is for compassionate

people who desire to serve the poor effectively. Drawn from the collective wisdom and experience of veteran servants who have spent good portions of their lives among the less fortunate, the principles provide a starting point for service. Just as the Hippocratic Oath provoked vigorous and sometimes heated debate among physicians and has required repeated modification to remain contemporary, this Oath for Compassionate Service will likely stimulate healthy discussion and adaptation appropriate for particular settings.

## The Oath for Compassionate Service

- Never do for the poor what they have (or could have) the capacity to do for themselves.

- Limit one-way giving to emergency situations.

- Strive to empower the poor through employment, lending, and investing, using grants sparingly to reinforce achievements.

- Subordinate self-interests to the needs of those being served.

- Listen closely to those you seek to help, especially to what is not being said—unspoken feelings may contain essential clues to effective service.

- Above all, do no harm.

Let's deal with these one by one.

## Never do for the poor what they have (or could have) the capacity to do for themselves.

Personal responsibility is essential for social, emotional, and spiritual well-being. To do for others what they have the capacity to do for themselves is to disempower them. The negative outcomes of welfare are no different when religious or charitable organizations provide it. The struggle for self-sufficiency is, like the butterfly struggling to emerge from its cocoon, an essential strength-building process that should not be short-circuited by "compassionate" intervention. The effective helper can be an encourager, a coach, a partner, but never a caretaker.

## Limit one-way giving to emergency situations.

Is the need crisis or chronic? Triage may be the appropriate intervention in an emergency situation, but it is hardly the strategy for a continuing need. The victims of a devastating tsunami need immediate medical attention, shelter, essential supplies, and hoards of volunteers. Over time, however, survivors' needs shift to expert consultation, a practical plan, and a combination of grants and loans to help them rebuild their destroyed community. Giving that continues beyond the immediate crisis produces diminishing returns.

Anyone who has served among the poor for any length of

time will recognize the following progression:

- give once and you elicit appreciation;
- give twice and you create anticipation;
- give three times and you create expectation;
- give four times and it becomes entitlement;
- give five times and you establish dependency.

While one-way giving may seem like the "Christian" thing to do, it can undermine the very relationship a helper is attempting to build. Such charity subtly implies that the recipient has nothing of value the giver desires in return. To the extent the poor are enabled to participate in the systems intended to serve them, their self-worth is enhanced.

**Strive to empower the poor through employment, lending, and investing, using grants sparingly to reinforce achievements.**

Lending to the poor establishes mutually beneficial relationships characterized by responsibility, accountability, and respect. It is a method of legitimate exchange that requires the lender to be responsible for assessing the risk while leaving the dignity of the borrower intact. Lending, done well, builds mutual trust and respect. Investing—making money *with* the poor—is the ultimate method of sharing resources (including expertise, connections, energy). It economically strengthens the poor through job-creating partnerships. Investing implies an ownership stake. To invest well with those who have limited access to capital requires a sound business plan, reasoned risk/reward ratio, adequate controls, and accountability. The investor has a stake in the sustainability and profitability of the venture. Grants are best used for R&D and gap funding to achieve sustainability.

**Subordinate self-interests to the needs of those being served.**

Organizational interests can subtly take precedence over the interests of the poor. When the agenda of a church is to create an inspiring, enriching, and well-planned mission experience for members, the real needs of the poor (like decent schools or stable employment) may be overlooked and dismissed as too complex or time consuming. Putting the front-burner agendas of those in need ahead of the self-interests of the helping organization may require considerable retooling, but it is a legitimate price for effective service.

**Listen closely to those you seek to help, especially to what is not being said—unspoken feelings may contain essential clues to effective service.**

The poor we serve may be reluctant to reveal "the whole story" to would-be helpers for a host of reasons—intimidation, fear of judgment, fear of losing support, fear of appearing unappreciative. A single mother trying to clothe her children will be hesitant to tell the clothes-closet volunteers that their hours of operation make it difficult for working parents to shop there. But like good physicians whose thorough examination yields an accurate diagnosis and treatment, effective helpers must learn to carefully observe behaviors, ask insightful questions, use their intuition, and hear what is not being said.

**Above all, do no harm.**

Every change has consequences. Church growth may cause traffic congestion; successful sheep breeding may lead to overgrazing. While we cannot foresee all the potential consequences of our service, we should at least make some attempt to predict its impact. Before we embark on any new service venture, we should conduct an "impact study" to consider how our good deeds might have unintended consequences. Are we luring indigenous ministers away from their pastoral duties to become schedule coordinators for our mission trips? Are we creating dependencies that may ultimately erode self-sufficiency? As Hippocrates admonished: *above all, do no harm.*

## Community Transformation

WE ALL LIVE IN communities. Healthy communities produce healthy offspring; dysfunctional communities perpetuate pathology. It becomes critically important, then, that efforts to transform the lives of the poor include intentional strategies for transforming their neighborhoods. This is community development, and it is distinctly different from community service. In community development, applying the principles of the Oath for Compassionate Service are fundamental.

In a recent survey of the one hundred fastest-growing churches in the United States, Rebecca Loveless, researcher for Discovery Church, Orlando, asked the question: Is your church engaged in community development ministry? All answered in the affirmative. But when asked to name their target neighborhood and their transformation goals, none was able to give a definitive answer. All were engaged in community service of various sorts, but none were focused on transforming a specific community.

As important as days-of-service work may be, they simply do not effect lasting change. What is required to transform a deteriorating neighborhood is *geographically focused vision* with *measurable goals* over *extended time*. Without a vision of what the transformed community will look like and a clearly defined strategy for getting there, sporadic, short-term volunteer service is likely to be little more than a well-intentioned, feel-good activity.

So what does a healthy community look like? Ask a senior, and she will likely recount childhood memories of laughing with classmates on their walk to and from school. And you will probably hear something like: "And we never had to lock our doors." Ask a young urban mother who must keep her children sequestered indoors or must train a vigilant eye on them every minute they are at play in the park. The response of these two women may be quite different, but the theme is the same. Safety is a top priority in a healthy neighborhood.

Good schools is another essential ingredient in a healthy community. In 2008 the suburban Atlanta Clayton County school district lost its accreditation due to a dysfunctional school board mired in petty politics. One result was a dramatic exodus. Like rats jumping off a sinking ship, middle-income families bailed in search of schools providing an acceptable level of education for their children. Lower-income families, like those who live in inner-city neighborhoods, had fewer options, staying where rents are cheap and education substandard.

Economic viability. Another essential. A community abandoned by upwardly mobile homeowners and left to absentee slumlords invites criminal activity and discourages legitimate business. Supermarkets leave, banks close, and struggling neighbors are left with high-priced convenience stores and predatory lenders. A healthy neighborhood, conversely, has sufficient disposable income to attract legitimate businesses that compete for a market share of community earnings.

Safety, decent schools, and a viable economy. There are doubtless a dozen or more other characteristics of a healthy community but these top the list. Without priority given to these three ingredients, community transformation is not likely to happen.

With issues so daunting, how do you even begin to make a significant impact?

First, don't presume that because an area is poor and run down it is devoid of leadership and resources. In every community there are leaders who exercise influence—informal leadership perhaps or elected officers of a not-so-well-organized neighborhood association, but leaders nonetheless. There are neighbors who know the history, know what's happening behind barred doors. There are dreamers and visionaries in those dilapidated houses, guardians of hope who keep the community from sliding into despair. If we ignore these leaders, we steamroll communities with our own programs. The first and most important step in community development, as we saw in Geralyn's work in Nicaragua, is to *listen*.

David VanCronkhite, inner-city minister and close friend, was not aware of the importance of recognizing community leadership when he first ventured into a housing project in our area. His idea was to win the hearts of ghetto children by bringing in a trailerload of ponies to ride. All seemed to be going well until the president of the tenants association showed up, cursed him out, and ordered him and his ponies off the property.

Stunned, David did as he was told. Only later did he realize that a good community leader must be cautious of strangers coming into her community to entice children with seemingly innocent fun. And even if the strangers meant no harm, who would be responsible to scoop up the poop on the playground when the ponies were gone?

Getting to know community leaders first requires us to *listen* and *respect* indigenous leadership and learn the *dreams* of the people. And be willing to have our own ideas transformed. Both the community and its leaders may have different goals from those that volunteers might bring. Instead of ponies, they may want an after-school program. Even if their aspirations seem low, even survival level, their ideas may still be good entry points for larger community development. An after-school homework program may develop into a partnership with the local school that ignites new energy and raises the quality of education for all the children of the community.

The entry point into community involvement is less important than the visions that hopeful volunteers can stimulate. They may begin with tutoring in the local school, or helping to organize a crime watch, or coaching a youth sports team. Such activities build trust and acquaint volunteers with the realities of the environment. The best investments, however, are not the programs volunteers initiate but the *capacity and connections of committed partners*. Achievers (as opposed to survivors) with access to resources have the capacity to lift their gaze above the dire realities of a struggling neighborhood and see paths to new possibilities. Dreams grow quickly when fueled by new possibilities. Their connections uniquely equip them to bring history-changing influences to bear upon the safety, education, and economic challenges of a community. This is what distinguishes community-developer partners from service-project volunteers.

## *Community Development Fundamentals*

COMMUNITY DEVELOPMENT IS A discipline, a school of thought, a unique approach to transforming underresourced neighborhoods or villages. Unlike relief work providing emergency assistance in crisis, community development focuses on chronically disadvantaged people and the places where they live. Sometimes referred to as asset-based community development, it is a positive approach that looks for existing assets rather than deficits, viewing a glass half full rather than half empty.

Community development is different from the model of *doing for* those in chronic need or starting a program to serve them. To begin with, it's more complex. It's an empowering philosophy that begins with the strengths (not problems) that poor communities already have and then builds upon those strengths. Also important, community development resists anything that would undermine the building of indigenous capacity. Enabling the poor to create their own solutions is obviously a much slower process than fixing problems for them—painfully slow for high-capacity friends with resources who would effect a quick "cure." In the final analysis, however, *doing for* people may actually prove to be hurtful.

While community development may begin with emergency relief, it immediately seeks ways to transition to development. Switzerland-based Medair, a faith-based nongovernmental organization (NGO) that responds to the world's most vulnerable people affected by crisis, exemplifies this practice. They bring life-saving relief and rehabilitation to disaster-stricken areas by working alongside local residents. Roger Sandberg, former Haiti country director, describes the progression as having three stops on a continuum: relief, rehabilitation, and development. "Defining these stops is an art rather than a science," Roger says.

- **First stop, relief.** *Relief work occurs during and immediately following an emergency and includes not only life-saving interventions but also the alleviation of suffering.*

- **Second stop, rehabilitation.** *Rehabilitation follows and overlaps with the relief phase. Rehabilitative work increases the capacity of a local community, enabling them to better respond to future crises. Rehabilitation also seeks to promote projects that restore services or livelihoods to a preexisting or improved level.*

- **Third stop, development.** *Development interventions follow and overlap relief and rehabilitation phases. Development work is long term. It seeks to improve the standard of living for a population over many years or decades. In the best-case scenario, relief and rehabilitation interventions are done with long-term development in mind.*

"Very roughly," continues Roger, "we might say that relief, rehabilitation, and development phases respectively last months, years, and decades."

Community development is a methodology designed to transform the poor, their families and their communities in sustainable and holistic ways. The following are some of the principles that guide this effort:

**1. Focus on community**—We are interdependent by design (economically, socially, spiritually). Growth and transformation is best realized in the context of community. Community is defined both as place (neighborhood or village) and human relationships (networks or cooperatives).

**2. Focus on assets**—Identify and build upon existing community strengths and resources, not on needs or limitations. Leverage the abilities and natural resources of individuals, communities, and/or the region to facilitate value-added opportunities. An asset-based approach encourages entrepreneurship.

**3. Focus on "front-burner" issues**—Begin with the important agendas of the community. When community residents are the first investors in a project, it gauges their level of priority and commitment. Economic sustainability and growth are goals for every activity. This helps establish the platform and trust to follow with initiatives for social and spiritual transformation.

**4. Focus on investing**—Whenever possible, invest with the poor to grow local assets and create wealth-generating opportunities. Appropriate lending is collateralized and has accountable repayment schedules. Grants should be in the form of incentives rather than charitable gifts.

**5. Focus on leadership development**—When the vision for community improvement is championed by indigenous leadership and when that leadership has the capacity to both organize and execute community projects, sustainable progress can be realized. Supporting local leadership builds capacity.

**6. Focus on pace—don't get ahead of the people**—As resourced outsiders, we must resist the temptation to "take over" a project. Local people must remain in control of their own development, which dictates the pace of progress. This creates true ownership and positions the community as being primarily responsible for the outcomes. Our best roles are as catalysts, facilitators, and connectors.

East Lake, one of the neighborhoods FCS has partnered with, illustrates the value of a focused approach. Once a resort community on the outskirts of Atlanta, East Lake by 1960 had deteriorated into a crime-ridden ghetto. Property values had plummeted, businesses had left, drugs and prostitution flourished. It had become a symbol of all that was wrong in the city.

Tom Cousins, fellow church member and successful real-estate developer, called one day with an outlandish idea—restore the defunct East Lake golf course to its former world-class status and use it as a catalyst to turn the community around. He had given generously to many causes over the years, he said, but this time he wanted to focus his philanthropy on a single location to see if lasting change could be accomplished. He was convinced that the once-famous golf course, home of golf legend Bobby Jones, was an asset that could be exploited for the benefit of the community. He would convert the golf course if FCS would work on community transformation, he challenged. I agreed.

The community's front-burner issue was crime. That's where we began. All the data pointed to three "hot spots"— two streets where criminal activity was nearly unchecked and, right in the middle of the neighborhood, a 650-unit public-housing project. The most effective methods for gaining the upper hand on crime are neighborhood watches and acquiring the real estate that criminals inhabit. Community organizing was the easier task. Buying up crack houses and converting public housing to private ownership was a bigger challenge. But with the help of lenders and investors, a long-neglected rental neighborhood began to emerge with new ownership and vitality. A forward-thinking housing authority director, excited by the vision, initiated the demolition of the troubled housing project and replaced it with a beautifully designed mixed-income apartment community.

It was clear that community leadership would not flourish without a quality school to educate tomorrow's leaders. It took herculean effort to persuade the Atlanta school board to approve a charter school for East Lake, but once accomplished, the way was cleared to hire top educators who, within two years, raised student performance from dead last to the top third in Atlanta public schools.

The golf course proved to be a cash cow for the community. Its exclusive membership attracted one hundred of the nation's wealthiest business leaders, and it landed the prestigious distinction of becoming the new permanent home of the PGA tour championship. Proceeds yielding up to $1 million a year finance a wide range of services, including a junior golf academy, tutoring, summer camps and clinics, community chaplaincy, and a host of other community-enhancing programs. East Lake is now one of Atlanta's most desirable, mixed-income, in-town neighborhoods. It serves as an example of how focused, visionary effort can have significant transformative impact.

The work of transforming communities and the people who live in them is a challenging, many-faceted process. And single-agenda programs are simply not up to the task. Developing and implementing a holistic plan that will turn a deteriorating neighborhood around takes multiple players (private, public, religious, and secular) with multiple funding streams. It requires a shared vision and much coordination.

A popular misconception is that collaboration is the key to community development. Essential as collaboration may be, it is simply not sufficient to effect community transformation.

## *When Collaboration Is Not Enough*

COLLABORATION. IN POLITICS, IT'S talking across the aisle. In religion, it's crossing denominations. In business, it's joint-venturing on a deal. In social service, it's cooperating for funding. Sounds good, right?

Apply for a government or philanthropic grant, and you will discover a definite bias in favor of organizations that work collaboratively with others. Funders are far more likely to support organizations working in concert with other important players in their community than lone rangers. For the most part, communities are healthier and outcomes are better when all the interests are represented at the table. For the most part.

Collaboration may be necessary for healthy community life, but it is not sufficient for community development. It would appear, on the surface at least, that well-coordinated delivery of services would enhance the quality of life in a community. If health agencies, for example, coordinated their services, the quality of healthcare would improve. Likely. Or if churches developed communication networks to monitor the distributions from their food pantries and clothes closets, accountability would increase and double-dipping would decrease. Probably. But such services, important as they may be, do not strengthen the fabric of a community. Services, even well-coordinated ones, do not make a community.

There is no question that collaboration offers highly attractive benefits—increased efficiency, economies of scale, elimination of duplication, and comprehensive service, to name a few. This is the compelling rationale of mergers and acquisitions. It also appeals to funders who would like to see the social-service "business" be more cost effective and efficient. The logic, of course, is that a more efficient delivery system will result in stronger, healthier communities.

But take the proliferation of the state-of-the-art Kroc multipurpose human-services centers being funded from the McDonald's empire. These centers, placed at in-town locations, are expansive, well designed, and bring together a broad range of public and private social-service agencies. This is a prime example of a foundation's belief in the value of collaboration.

It is also a prime example of the erroneous belief that better-coordinated services make healthier communities. The approach fails to consider the negative impact on the surrounding neighborhood when hundreds of addicted, troubled, delinquent, or homeless clients from a wide area converge on a single location. If the Kroc "collaboration logic" were true, then those neighborhoods with the highest concentration of social-service agencies would be the healthiest. In fact, the opposite is true.

John McKnight, founder of the widely accepted Asset-Based Community Development movement, says this: "I've been around neighborhoods, neighborhood organizations, and communities in big cities for thirty-six years. I have never seen service systems that brought people to well-being, delivered them to citizenship, or made them free."

His extensive research concludes that services rarely empower the poor because (1) they divert money away from poor people to service providers, (2) programs are based on deficiencies rather than capacities, and (3) services displace the ability of people's organizations to solve problems. However worthy their intentions, McKnight believes, collaborative efforts of organizations may actually serve to disempower the poor.

He and others in community development ask for honest answers to these penetrating questions:

- Does the proposed activity strengthen the capacity of neighborhood residents to prioritize and address their own issues?

- Will the proposed activity be wealth-generating or at least self-sustaining for the community?

- Do the moneys generated for and/or by local residents remain at work in their community?

- Does the proposed activity have a timetable for training and transferring ownership to indigenous leadership?

Such questions go to the heart of capacity building rather than service providing. These are not "needs survey" questions to identify deficits. Rather, they assume that there are untapped potential and underutilized assets in the community waiting to be mobilized. Community development's aim is to strengthen capacity rather than focus on providing services.

If collaboration is to ultimately benefit the community, it must be guided by ultimate outcomes. When an outcomes approach combines collaboration and community development, these can become effective allies. When community residents, local businesses, educators, and entrepreneurs come together to discuss important issues and develop action plans, community capacity increases. The community is then in a position to identify those additional resources required (which may include service agencies) to enable them to accomplish their goals.

## CHAPTER NINE

# *Service with Dignity*

ATTENTIVE LISTENING COMMUNICATES WORTH; LEGITI-
MATE employment gives meaning to life; community gives a
sense of belonging—all three enhance human dignity. The
following interactions describe how these play out among diverse urban neighbors.

Effective service among the less privileged requires a significant degree of awareness and delicacy. Sometimes even
the most innocent and well-meaning attempts to help, inflict
pain. Made in the image of God, we are created with intrinsic worth. And anything that erodes a rightful sense of pride
and self-respect diminishes that image. At best we are fragile, easily wounded by criticism or insult. But those who have
been devalued by society are unusually sensitive to the sig-
nals they receive from the dominant culture. Those in service
work have the responsibility to listen to what those in need are

saying and—as the Oath of Compassionate Service states—also to what is not being said. Herein lie essential clues that help us provide effective care. Listen in on a conversation I had with one of my neighbors.

"I hate it when volunteers come down here," Virgil muttered, just loud enough for me to hear. We were sitting on my front porch steps as a white fourteen-passenger van crept past. We didn't need to read the lettering on the side to know that it was a church van—the smiling, light-skinned youth waving from the windows told us that. Virgil's reaction surprised me. A church group had invested $20,000 and eight weekends of labor to build his home. Another one had helped him purchase and install attractive landscaping. I assumed his response to volunteers would be positive.

Bewildered, I asked him why. "Do you know what it's like to have people look down on you like you're poor, like you need help?" he said. "I know they're just trying to be nice but, damn, they insult you and don't even know it! Like one lady mentioned to me and Tamara how clean our house was. I guess she thought it was a compliment. What she was really saying was 'I'm surprised to see your house isn't infested with roaches and filled with trash like most black families.' A couple people told me how smart and well-behaved my kids were, surprised that they weren't dumb and rowdy like most inner-city black kids. I see through their words. I hear what they really think.

"But," he continued, "you have to keep smiling and act like you don't know what's going on. I really hate it!"

It had taken five years for Virgil to reach this level of candor with me, five years of being neighbors, raising our kids together, being in each other's homes. Had he been a less secure man, these highly personal feelings would likely have remained concealed in the closed domain of his and Tamara's private lives. Especially considering that I was one of his white benefactors. I was the one who orchestrated the construction of his home, mobilized church volunteers, raised the money. I knew Virgil was grateful to have a permanent home for his family—he expressed it many times.

What I didn't realize until this day on my front porch steps was the price he had paid to be a recipient of my charity, the damage it had inflicted on his manly pride. Nor would I ever have known had we not become neighbors and trusted friends.

Virgil's honesty and candor caused us to revise our ministry, prompting a marked changed in our approach. My first attempt at corrective action was to conduct sensitivity training for volunteers in preparation for their service projects. If caring people realized that their charitable efforts, though very important to the poor, took a toll on the self-esteem of those being helped, they would be more sensitive.

Made aware of subliminal attitudes and messages they inadvertently (and innocently) communicated, service workers and volunteers could avoid unintentional insults, I reasoned. But my reasoning didn't work. Not the way I intended, at any rate.

Conversations once cheerful and upbeat, naively so, now

became cautious and controlled. Taking care not to offend, communication became uneasy and restrained for volunteers.

I had another talk with Virgil. "Should we even invite volunteers to come into our community to serve?" I asked. They make a big difference, Virgil reminded me. Building affordable homes for those who would likely never be able to own a home, repairing widows' porches and roofs, counseling at summer camp, helping to build a community playground . . . the list was long. Yes, we had benefited greatly from the investments of volunteers.

"But," I said, "if other neighbors reacted viscerally at the sight of a church van the way you did, there is obviously something wrong with our approach."

"Maybe neighbors would react differently if they were the ones doing the inviting." What if, before any volunteers were scheduled, neighbors met together to discuss community needs, decided which were highest priority, identified available resources within the community, and then decided what (if any) outside support they needed? That way volunteers could come in as reinforcements for a community-driven effort, work under the direction of neighborhood leadership, and celebrate together their mutual accomplishments. Community driven rather than volunteer driven, community led rather than volunteer led.

"But what about the demeaning attitudes of well-meaning volunteers?" I continued.

"Folks in the hood know what's going on," Virgil reminded

me. "Blacks know a lot more about whites than whites know about blacks—that's survival. Trying to get rich white folk to change their deep-seated views by putting on a one- or two-hour sensitivity class isn't going to change anyone. That kind of change takes years of close relationships. No, it's better just to let the neighborhood do the inviting, and maybe talk together about the cost of accepting charity from good people who aren't aware of how insulting they can be. If neighbors agree that the price is worth the help, then they'll welcome the volunteers and let honest friendships develop naturally over time if they're going to."

And so our volunteer strategy changed once again. Awareness raising for volunteers still remains an important aspect of service projects, but the most important understandings come in the context of candid conversations with those in the communities served. Guided discussions over lunch, on worksites, or in the homes of community residents provide excellent settings. When residents have the opportunity to tell their stories, share how their faith has sustained them during difficult times, and pray for their visiting friends, the volunteers' "pity factor" diminishes, replaced by respect and emerging understanding.

Engaging the community in prioritizing and planning the work has also become a prerequisite for mutually satisfying service projects. And employing community residents to lead, supervise, and teach their visiting guests continues to affirm the dignity of indigenous leadership.

For this, too, I can thank my friend Virgil.

## *Good Work*

LITTLE AFFIRMS HUMAN DIGNITY more than honest work. One of the surest ways to destroy self-worth is subsidizing the idleness of able-bodied people. Work is a gift, a calling, a human responsibility. And the creation of productive, meaningful employment fulfills one of the Creator's highest designs. Because of that, it should be a central goal to our service.

Some time ago I had a major landscaping job ahead of me. A fire had destroyed a neighbor's home some months back. The vacant lot was cleared of the larger rubble, but tall grass and weeds had taken over, concealing shards of glass, rusted car parts, chunks of concrete, half-melted wire—the sort of debris that made mowing impossible. I decided to take on the project—a full day of work—and assumed I could round up some labor. I blocked out Monday in my schedule.

On that early-morning Home Depot run as I was loading grass seed and wheat straw into my pickup, I glanced across the parking lot and saw a group of men, perhaps thirty of them, clustered near the street entrance. Day laborers waiting for work—just what I needed. I headed over toward their assembly area intending to do a little negotiating. The group appeared to be somewhat orderly, snaking in an irregular line, those near the front poised for the next "boss" to arrive and signal for the number of workers he needed for the day. I would need two.

As I drove in the direction of the group, I was immediately aware that every eye was glued on my pickup. I had not come to a full stop when the line of men broke into a running, jostling mob that surrounded my truck. Eager faces pressed against every window, each intent on capturing my attention. "I'm a good worker . . . Me? I'm a professional landscaper . . . I work hard . . . Me? take me"—dozens of loud, urgent voices simultaneously overtalking one another. I scanned the horde of pushing, elbowing humanity—unshaven Caucasians in sweat-stained ball caps, black men with braids protruding beneath stocking caps, raven-haired men speaking broken English—every one desperate for a day's work.

I randomly pointed to two young Hispanic men who had worked their way to my driver's-side window. "You two, jump in the back," I yelled loud enough to be heard over the clamor. Stepping out of the truck, I began to negotiate a wage with the two men now sitting on the hay bales in the back of my truck. "How much?" I asked. "Ten dollars," they responded. Agreed.

Other men still pressed around me as I jumped back into the driver's seat. "One more worker? Me too?" An African American, seeing he had been bypassed for two Mexicans, indicted me: "You ain't no American." As I pulled away, in my rearview mirror I saw the faces of two men who continued to follow my truck, clinging to the fading hope that I might need one more worker for the day.

Strong, able-bodied men, up early in the morning, eager to work, willing to do menial labor for minimal pay. What inner drive compelled them to endure such a prideless contest? Overdue rent? Child support? Families back in Mexico? Alcohol? The responses would have varied greatly, I know. But none would have revealed the underlying motivation: meaning. Life offers no fulfillment without work.

Our earliest glimpse of the cosmos is a creative God at work. And the original design of paradise pictures humanity at work. Work is fundamentally a cosmic activity. As Matthew Fox claims in *The Reinvention of Work*, it is "the" cosmic activity. "There is only one work in the cosmos . . . that one work is God's work. Humans are invited to participate." Rafael and Juan, riding on hay bales in the back of my pickup, wind blowing through their hair, chosen to participate in God's good work. No matter the task. Clearing debris from a lot or running a corporation, mopping the kitchen floor or selling a piece of real estate. Work, all work, is an invitation from God for us to take an active role as coparticipants in an ever-unfolding creation.

### Good Neighbors

EVEN AS WORK IS essential for life with meaning, so neighboring is essential for meaningful community life. Becoming a neighbor to less-advantaged people is the most authentic expression of affirmation I know—becoming a real-life, next-door neighbor. When connected neighbors move into the struggling world of those who are poor in order to be friends (rather than profit-making gentrifiers), new possibilities begin to appear. With resourced neighbors come educational improvements, better stores, safer streets. Is it unreasonable to think that faith-motivated young professionals might eagerly respond to the invitation to become strategic neighbors if they were issued an invitation?

Young people ready and willing to sacrifice for a worthy cause are hardly a scarcity.

I see them every day as I drive past the high school across from my office, standing stiffly at attention in tight rows and columns, smartly dressed. It's ROTC morning inspection and drill. Students—teenagers—preparing to enter the U.S. military. Their commanding officer is a career soldier who understands the vital importance of discipline, commitment, training. The marching, the commands, the rigors of physical training are all essential preparation for a combat-ready army. As soon as they graduate from high school, these young recruits will join thousands of other volunteers to become a proud fighting force ready at a moment's notice to be shipped out for duty anywhere in the world.

What motivates these young people to willingly choose to put themselves in harm's way? Adventure? A noble cause? A career? No draft compels them into military service. They are free to choose safer paths, choices that would not require leaving family behind. But every day lines of them file into the recruitment office to sign up, knowing full well the likelihood that they will be deployed into battle.

Whether we agree with the wars in Iraq and Afghanistan, we nevertheless support and applaud troops in our airports, we recognize them in the news, we celebrate their homecoming. Young men and women who sacrifice for causes we believe in. If not the policies, surely their patriotism deserves affirmation and respect.

An all-volunteer military of nearly two and a half million active and reserve troops demonstrates conclusively one significant point: young people will offer themselves sacrificially to a cause and a country they believe in. Is it not reasonable to assume that young people of faith will also give themselves sacrificially to a mission worthy of their best for a kingdom and mission they believe in?

Deteriorating urban neighborhoods suffer from the relentless exodus of their most able neighbors. For these communities to be reborn, new capable, connected neighbor leaders must return. All that is required to ignite such a vision is an appeal to some of our best and brightest young people to become on-the-ground visionaries and stake out a beachhead in a troubled area. And it is not an unrealistic expectation.

"Reneighboring" is a primary transformation strategy of FCS. Scores of dedicated young (and not so young) visionaries have moved into our target neighborhoods to become neighbors alongside long-time residents who have endured years of neglect. And there are many inspiring examples of churches and ministries employing this "reneighboring" approach to community rebirth. The Christian Community Development

Association (ccda.org) is a national movement involving thousands of dedicated, frontline "troops" who—somewhat like a service corps—have moved into neighborhoods of need, engaged in collective action with their neighbors, confronted destructive influences, and turned entire communities around.

Christ United Methodist Church in Memphis is a stellar example. This large, in-town congregation became concerned about the deplorable living conditions in the Binghampton neighborhood, a long-neglected area a stone's throw from the church. They adopted it as their parish and mobilized their members to begin outreach there. They began with volunteer service projects repairing seniors' homes. But a significant ministry shift took place when two of the young church families bought homes in Binghampton and moved in. Soon these frontline "marines" were engaged in all manner of community issues—safety, education, drugs, slumlords—the same conditions long-time neighbors had struggled with for years. But unlike their low-income neighbors, these newcomers had connections—a strong, committed, well-resourced church.

Soon several dilapidated houses were acquired, rehabbed, and occupied by additional strategic neighbors recruited and commissioned by the church. The impact on Binghampton was immediately noticeable. Crime rates began to decline, a drug house boarded up, the quality of life showed signs of improvement. Others signed up for the mission and moved in. Their numbers grew to forty. Binghampton Development Corporation was then created to provide skilled leadership to initiate a comprehensive redevelopment plan. At last count, seventy households relocated to the neighborhood, providing leadership to create a health clinic and a school.

The strategy requires someone with vision to raise a flag and give these marching orders: "Love God and love your neighbor." In order to understand the culture, win the hearts and minds of residents, and plan an effective campaign, special forces must be sent in to become indigenized. Call them strategic neighbors. They are called, courageous, and highly committed. They have the people skills that allow them to move easily among diverse populations, gathering intelligence and building authentic relationships as they go. They instinctively inspire and mobilize locals to assert positive leadership on their streets. They know what type of reinforcements to call in and when. And these valorous ones are among us: in our churches and on our college campuses, waiting to receive their commission.

Churches often have a ready reserve of talented recruits. With a defined parish (target neighborhood) and a focused vision, a church becomes a natural place for transformative relationships. Consider the range of reinforcements a church can supply when members are deployed and relocate into a struggling community. They become tutors for children having difficulty keeping up in school, coaches for neighborhood athletic teams, counselors for summer camp, real estate agents to track down the owners of crack houses, lawyers to structure LLCs to acquire distressed or foreclosed properties, investors to form real estate investment funds, construction professionals and handyman volunteers to rehab houses.

I can't get the image out of my mind of those ROTC cadets, standing at attention, brass shining, shoes gleaming, ready to serve their nation proudly. Much closer than Afghanistan or Iraq are local organizations and ministries waging peace where fear and violence reign. Reports of the bloodshed are broadcast daily in the local news. Nearby are battles that can be won.

The guidebook for strategic neighbors has yet to be written. So when young professionals and ministries feel called to relocate into communities of need, they seek out others who have gone before them. One Miami couple, John and Leneita Fix, recently moved into the neighborhood where many of the children in their inner-city youth program live. Committed to becoming strategic neighbors, they were eager to learn all they could about living in a cross-cultural environment. We met for lunch to discuss their challenges.

"So what do we do now?" Leneita asked me as our lunch was being served up. Since Peggy and I moved our family into the city thirty-plus years ago, we have been sought out by many couples who felt a similar calling, especially those with children. Where did your kids go to school? Did you get a dog or a burglar-alarm system? How did you control the flow of neighborhood kids in and out of your house? Important issues for suburban families entering a new culture.

John and Leneita have the distinct advantage of already

having good relationships with some of their new neighbors. And the stress of transition will likely be mild for their three children, who already know some of the neighborhood kids and have picked up a fair amount of street smarts through their involvement at the ministry center. The larger question on John and Leneita's minds was how to have a transformative impact on their new community. Should they do a neighborhood needs assessment or start a tutoring program in the local school or . . . . The list of possibilities was considerable. Where should they begin?

"Don't initiate anything," I told them. Not at first. Be a learner. Ask a million questions. Learn your neighbors' names, kids, church membership (if any), where they work, what they like or dislike about the neighborhood, the history, who knows whom. Meet the school principal, the city-council representative, the police-precinct captain, local merchants, PTA president, pastors. Find out what is happening in the community from their unique perspectives. Attend community-association meetings, public hearings, church services, high school athletic events, local art and musical performances. Meet with city planning staff and find out what if any plans the city has on the drawing board for your community. In short, become an expert on your community. Immerse yourselves in every aspect of community life. Volunteer as appropriate, but make no long-term commitments. Be an interested, supportive neighbor for *at least six months* before attempting to initiate any new activity.

Listen attentively, and you will discover that almost everyone has an opinion to offer. If neighbors perceive that you value their insights, they are likely to reveal volumes of important information. By assuming the position of a learner in search of valuable information about your new community, you affirm the knowledge base of neighbors, be they seniors with a wealth of history to share, moms who know where to find quality day care, school teachers who understand local educational assets and challenges, or business owners who have the pulse on local economics. People feel valued when their insights are taken seriously. And everyone has important intelligence to contribute.

On the other hand, neighbors are much less likely to be receptive to bright, confident newcomers who come with "solutions" to the visible problems of the community. Such newcomers may indeed bring good ideas and much needed resources. But they may also overlook valuable assets that already exist within the community, assets needed to sustain positive change. In so doing, they inadvertently devalue the community and communicate a subtle attitude of superiority. That's why it is far better to enter the neighborhood as a learner than an initiator. For any capable, mission-driven urban practitioner eager to change the world, this will feel counterintuitive, but it is a discipline worth developing.

The discussion with John and Leneita continued. Six months of focused learning yields a remarkably accurate picture of the realities of your new home. In six months you can meet most of the community influencers (both formal and informal) and gather current data on homeownership, property values, educational levels, crime stats, economic activity, and political currents. Then, with a realistic assessment of the potentials and obstacles of your environment, you are better prepared to make strategic decisions about your involvement in community life.

Your "bigger picture" perspective will allow you to establish personal priorities well suited to your unique gift sets. Leneita may be drawn toward educational involvement, strengthening the PTA, establishing a tutoring program, or even running for the school board. John may become involved in affordable housing, help organize a nonprofit community-development corporation or take on zoning issues. Or you may conclude that, given your family demands, you need to invest heavily on your street to ensure that it becomes a healthy place for children to grow up.

But in making such decisions, one thing is vitally important to remember: *need does not constitute a call*! There are far more needs in a poor neighborhood than any one family can begin to address. And those needs, like the Sirens' call to Odysseus, will attempt to lure you to them, only to pull you off course, consume your schedule, and deplete your energy. Focus your efforts in one or two areas that have a compelling interest to you, that maximize your giftedness. Defining (narrowing) your involvement allows you to concentrate your best energies strategically while establishing the boundaries that allow you to limit the host of other pressing priorities that call out to you. Your marriage and family life will thank you. And your community will ultimately appreciate the presence of a healthy family and an effective neighbor.

# Chapter Ten

## *Getting Started*

This book would be incomplete without offering a few practical steps toward transformative charity. While the scope and scale of charity is vast, the on-the-ground experience of this urban practitioner is largely limited to inner-city settings and poor communities in underdeveloped countries. Thus, the next steps suggested in this concluding chapter apply more directly to church groups, service organizations, and volunteer involvement than to macroeconomic and government-aid policies. The following suggestions, like the needle of a compass, point in the direction of responsible aid but are hardly a detailed road map. They point the way from "betterment" toward "development."

When a neighborhood has suffered from years of neglect, when trash has piled up on vacant lots, when the city no longer replaces shot-out street lights or fixes potholes, almost any outside help is welcome. Even eager youth from suburban churches who arrive on Saturday mornings to fill dumpsters with old tires and collect mounds of debris in garbage bags are welcome. Seniors, peering from behind window blinds, are grateful that something—anything—positive is taking place on their streets.

Parents of latchkey kids seek healthy alternatives to the destructive influences of the street and are eager for after-school programs to augment inadequate public education. They need safe places for the children while they are at work. The underfunded Boys & Girls Clubs in tired old facilities are important but insufficient. And the seniors, many too frail to keep up their homes, need someone to help fix leaking roofs and repair rotting porches.

For volunteers desiring to make a difference, this is the ideal place to focus. Tutoring, weekend service projects, summer-camp counseling, sports programs—these and a host of other hands-on activities can make a significant difference in the lives of kids and seniors and help ease the load for struggling parents.

This kind of high-touch involvement is what we call "betterment." Betterment offers immediate relief. It improves existing conditions. Indigenous neighbors often attempt such efforts sacrificially, but their resources are limited. Thus, many betterment programs are initiated by and dependent upon the goodwill of outsiders. Recipients admittedly sacrifice some self-esteem, but for many it is a price worth paying.

Betterment programs do make a difference. Yet, as important as these services may be (essential, some would say), serving people is distinctly different from developing people.

- Betterment does for others. Development maintains the long view and looks to enable others to do for themselves.

- Betterment improves conditions. Development strengthens capacity.

- Betterment gives a man a fish. Development teaches a man how to fish.

Most poverty programs begin as betterment. When we realize that we have the capacity (and the responsibility) to meet a need, we naturally look for the most direct and immediate way to intervene. A homeless man is hungry, so we offer him food. A bright child is failing in school, so we help her with her homework. An aging widow's heat has been cut off, so we pay her gas bill. These are personal acts of compassion that address an immediate, correctable need.

Then we discover that there are many more hungry people out there, many educationally disadvantaged children and neglected seniors. Our hearts may compel us to do more. We look for methods that are more efficient than a one-on-one approach. We organize food drives, tutoring classes, and adopt-a-grandparent programs that expand our capacity to touch many more people in need. We envision strategies to eliminate hunger entirely in a community, to raise the standard of education for all area students, or to see that every homebound elder has a caring volunteer. This is the ground in which prototype ministry models spring up.

But superbly run betterment programs do little to strengthen the community's capacity to address its own needs. And often they can work at cross-purposes with community development. They are entry points but not ending points.

## Starting Points

"How did you select your target neighborhood?" It's a question churches ask us when they are considering making a commitment to a specific geographic area. Focused Community Strategies (FCS) in Atlanta makes a very intentional, long-term investment in a single neighborhood until significant transformation occurs. It sometimes takes a decade or more to effect lasting change. We are now in our fifth community.

"Is there a strategy you use to determine where to begin?" people ask, or "What community will you move to next?" Through unique sets of circumstances we have been drawn to each inner-city Atlanta community where we have served.

Our work in Grant Park began because it was central to many of the youth and families we were working with. A few of our staff had already relocated there, and a vacant church building was made available for our use.

Eventually our focus expanded to adjacent Summerhill, informally at first as Summerhill residents became involved in our church programs, then formally when we were invited by community leaders to assist in shaping a neighborhood revitalization plan.

Then the availability of a large tract of land in adjacent Ormewood Park induced us to attempt the development of a mixed-income subdivision.

The catalyst for involvement in East Lake, our fourth neighborhood, was a request from visionary real-estate developer Tom Cousins to partner with him in a total community transformation, the centerpiece being the restoration of a defunct golf course.

South Atlanta, where we are focused at the time of this book's release, came about as a result of a group of seniors who prevailed upon their city-council representative to set up a meeting with us. They had been praying for years, they said, that God would send them a partner who could help them turn their deteriorating community around.

There is no clear-cut formula to our decision-making process. In retrospect, it has been fortunate that all of our target neighborhoods have been located in the same general area of inner-city Atlanta—the southeast section. Three of them are contiguous. Two are separated by a mile or so from the others. We have discovered that there are distinct advantages to working in neighborhoods of close proximity. The "propinquity effect" (nearness of time, space, and relationship) reduces travel time, centralizes office space and administrative support, and permits easy staff interaction. A "contagion effect" also helps build momentum as reignited economic life tends to spread from one community to the next.

But back to the question of beginnings. When organizations and churches are looking for a starting point, I refer them to the words of author Henry Blackaby: find out what God is up to, and get in on it. There is no shortage of needs in most communities, especially poor ones, but the need does not constitute the call. Every vision requires a visionary, one who has the passion and energy to go on the point, to lead the charge. Without visionary drive and persistence, a mission that begins well can run out of gas when the work becomes tedious and the results slow in coming. Identifying and joining energies with a trusted visionary leader increases the chances of lasting impact.

Ask yourself: What is my parish? Historically, churches have had vested interests in their surrounding communities. And members often lived within walking distance of the church (explaining small parking lots). Pastors lived in the parsonages attached to or near the churches, and the churches had vital roles in the life of their communities. As a society, when we became commuterized churchgoers, all that changed. Most churches have lost their community roots, with little connection to the geography surrounding their buildings.

With gentrification rearranging the demographics of both cities and suburbs, now may be the opportune time to reconnect with our neighborhoods. Poverty is suburbanizing. People of different hues and languages are gravitating into once quiet suburban communities, seeking opportunities for employment and reasonably priced housing. This provides a strategic opportunity for churches to assess the changes going on around them and take a leadership role in serving their immediate parishes.

A pastor from a large suburban church came to my office to discuss this gentrification "concern" that was taking place in his area. His church had been a very active partner with us, building a dozen or more affordable homes for needy families in our neighborhood. "Your people are moving into our community," he told me, "and there is some real ambivalence about it." When "the problems of the city" began to show up in the classrooms and bus stops of their peaceful community, anxiety and fear began to surface. "How do we deal with this?" The pastor's question was an honest one.

As much as I hoped they would continue to partner with us, I told him, it was important to modify their outreach and refocus on the new neighbors God was bringing to them. The sixty-unit apartment complex within a block of their church might be an ideal location to begin. They could acquire the property, lease it to younger folks in their congregation, and leave a generous portion (one third, I suggested) of the apartments for "my people" who were moving into the area. This way the church could set an example of hospitality and become agents of reconciliation within their own community.

It was obviously a major shift for the church to consider, one that would require new organizational structures and different types of financing. Owing to strong, visionary pastoral leadership, they did in fact make that turn. It was a decision that refocused them on their local parish.

Focus is also essential if we expect measurable results. Define the parish too large, spread our ministry too thin, and we dissipate our energies. Tight geographic focus gives definition and boundaries to the mission. We may not be able to impact the entire public school system, but we can make a difference in one local elementary school. We may not reduce the crime rate of the metropolitan area, but we can take back a neighborhood, one crack house at a time, one block at a time.

Should we be blessed with success in our mission, our capacity for expansion will increase. This is both a blessing and a temptation. An educational program, for example, when its effectiveness becomes recognized, will inevitably be invited to expand to other schools. The broader the service area, however, the thinner our ability to have an impact at the street level.

And if we are committed to a local community, how do we measure community transformation? In South Atlanta, the inner-city neighborhood our ministry is currently focused on, a seven-year longitudinal study has been conducted. A foundation granting a significant sum to support our community-development plan wanted some objective measures on the effectiveness of their investment. They made a separate grant to a research organization to gather baseline data on the status of the neighborhood when we began our work and an update of that data annually over a seven-year period. There are six categories the Community Design Center of Atlanta determined to be indices for measuring community health:

- Public safety
- Educational improvements
- Economic vitality
- Homeowner/renter retention
- Neighborhood associations
- Spiritual vitality

Each of these categories is statistically measurable, though some are more difficult than others to cleanly define. Home occupancy and crime statistics are easily quantified. Spiritual vitality is harder to measure, but church attendance and participation in ministry activities give some indication. It is also impossible to determine what changes are the direct results of our involvement. What this study does do well, however, is define a very specific geographic area, chart the changes that occur over time, and channel our activities toward specific outcomes. At the end of the day, if we have fulfilled our mission, the health of the community should be significantly improved.

Community development has far too many facets for any one organization to tackle single-handedly, so focus becomes essential as organizations take form. In addition to having *geo-*

*graphic* focus, *activity* focus is also an important consideration. No one organization has the expertise to address all the challenges of a struggling community. Partnering with other organizations with specialized missions is essential for a holistic development strategy. But while single-agenda partners can contribute much, their zeal for their own mission can sometimes complicate matters. Understandably, mission-driven organizations tend to view their specific mission as the top priority. Habitat for Humanity is on a mission to provide affordable housing for every needy family. Imagine Schools has its sights set on transforming public education. The Union Mission seeks to reduce homelessness and addiction. All are important, along with a host of other equally redemptive programs. But without a balanced community-centric plan (as opposed to program-centric), programs can expand like cancer in unhealthy ways.

For example, it is very possible for Habitat to build too many affordable homes in a neighborhood, limiting the potential for the community to emerge with a healthy economic mix. Or a drug-treatment program might erect a large facility to satisfy its economies-of-scale requirements but end up necessitating the importing of addicted people from around the city. Loading an area down with poverty programs and human services can virtually ruin its chances of economic rebirth. A "master development plan" is needed to prioritize and coordinate a balanced involvement of partnering groups to protect the long-term vision for a restored, economically viable community. And big-picture visionary leadership is a gift of inestimable worth.

To be strategic is to prepare and execute an *effective* plan of action. The best way to assure effectiveness is to spend enough time as a learner, ask enough questions, and seek wisdom from indigenous leaders to gain an accurate picture of both existing realities and future aspirations of the community. Then, having made a realistic assessment of the time and asset commitment you (or your organization or church) can invest, offer low-visibility support to community-led activities. A patient, sensitive entry into grass-roots involvement can open future opportunities to assume a larger strategic role in transforming a neighborhood.

Timing is everything. When the decision has been made to shift emphasis from betterment to development and a partnership with a specific community is being considered, two questions inevitably arise: Are we ready for this and is the neighborhood ready? The following may provide useful guidelines for answering these questions.

Like most urban ministries, FCS began its involvement in the inner city, offering betterment programs. In time, however, the need for a more comprehensive, transformative strategy became apparent. The organization gradually evolved from a small nonprofit human-services program into a comprehensive community-development organization. By trial and error it developed a set of criteria to help determine if and when the timing was right to begin a new community partnership.

The ministry now goes only where it is invited by community leadership and then only when there is a commitment to development, including spiritual, economic, and social dimensions. It does not offer merely programs; rather, it provides a total redevelopment strategy. Before making a commitment to partner with a new neighborhood, the ministry asks the following series of questions. Only if the answer to most is "yes" and there is dedicated leadership available to lead the mission will FCS move forward.

- Is capable, indigenous (or indigenizing) visionary leadership behind the effort?

- Is the plan neighborhood-specific? Does it focus on one and only one target community?

- Is the effort comprehensive? Do the programmatic pieces all have as a primary objective the ultimate self-sufficiency of the neighborhood?

- Does the plan emanate from local churches and/or people of faith? (People of faith are the greatest resource of hope and vision within any community.)

- Does the plan protect against displacement or reconcentration of lower-income residents?

- Does the plan promote interdependency rather than continued dependency?

- Does the plan attract, retain, and/or develop indigenous leadership in the community?

- Does the plan attract new achieving neighbors into the community?

- Does the plan utilize grants and nonprofits as catalysts for development that can eventually reduce the need for external subsidies?

- Does the plan lead to economic neighborhood viability, as measured by its ability to attract and harness market forces?

## Knowing Your ABCDs

OUR PERCEPTIONS ABOUT A community influence our expectations. What we believe about a neighborhood will in large measure determine what we find when we arrive. View it as a dangerous ghetto and we will see drug dealers and prostitutes. See it as a "field of dreams" and vacant houses become investment opportunities. John McKnight, creator of the Asset-Based Community Development movement, gives important insights into the importance of focusing on potential rather than problems.

John was being introduced to a group of urban workers that had gathered to glean from his years of learning. The master of ceremonies presented John with little fanfare, a sparse introduction of few words. By prearrangement, John had requested that he be given the opportunity to introduce himself to the group.

He began: "Hello, I'm John McKnight, and as you can see," he tilted his head downward exposing a thinning scalp, "I'm going bald." He then removed his glasses and, holding them up for us to observe, explained: "My eyes are getting worse—at my last examination my eyesight was 20/100." He then pulled up his shirt, exposing a large scar on his abdomen, and continued: "I have had several surgeries over the years. This scar is from . . ." the litany went on. The audience, unsure whether this was bizarre humor or a loss of faculties, exchanged bewildered glances. John continued: "Let me tell you about some of the jobs I have lost," and he proceeded to describe several disappointing employment experiences. By this time everyone was smiling and chuckling, knowing that John was not at all deranged but rather shrewdly bringing home a point.

Of course we don't introduce ourselves this way. John dropped his act and got to the point of his introduction. We lead with our accomplishments, our degrees, our titles. We want people to think well of us, respect us, believe in our competence. Why then do we introduce our urban neighborhoods in the most negative light? Murder capital, highest school drop-out rate, drug infested, epidemic teen pregnancy . . . or whatever other claim to infamy we can use as "bragging" rights.

Well, we all knew the answer to John's rhetorical question. Fund-raising. Making things sound bad is how we tug on peoples' heartstrings and get them to give. People respond to tragedy, to extreme need. If our neighborhood has the worst infestation of crack houses in the city or the highest rate of child prostitution, something simply *must* be done about it. Marketing misfortune works. But there are other reasons for portraying the inner city in a bad light. There is a certain amount of ego satisfaction in being known as frontline troops who place themselves in harm's way to liberate a territory taken over by an evil force. The marines have used this as a recruitment strategy for years. The worse the enemy, the higher the praise. The greater the danger, the sweeter the rewards. To the conquerors go the spoils. Marines have bragging rights.

But when we mainly look on the negative aspects of a community, we overlook the capable leaders, the dedicated teachers, the legitimate business entrepreneurs, the good parents, the wise grandmothers. When we focus on what is wrong, we miss what is right. And our strategies for helping are driven by combating problems rather than strengthening potential.

But slip on the hat of the local neighborhood-association president. See the view of the street looking out the window of the community center. Look at the vacant lot the city just cleared, the dangerous burnt-out shell bulldozed and grass now starting to grow. Think about how much time and effort it took to mobilize residents to persistently call their city-council representative until the city took action. And look at the Ms. Martha's Day Care sign on the house just down the street. Remember the concerted action of neighbors to lobby city hall for a special use permit so this needed service could be started? And look at the colorful Neighborhood Reunion banner that stretches across the main street, and think of all the committees that are engaged in pulling off this event—the food committee, publicity committee, vender committee, entertainment committee, program committee, setup and cleanup committees . . . a seemingly endless list. This community teems with energy and life.

What we look for is likely what we will see. That's why John McKnight emphasizes *assets* in his *Asset-Based* Community Development philosophy. ABCD is welcome news to our urban neighbors who, in spite of significant challenges, exert valiant efforts to restore wholesomeness to their communities.

## So What Do We Do Next?

COMPASSIONATE PEOPLE DESIRE TO see wholeness restored to struggling communities and to the people who reside there. But as explored previously, betterment programs of many service organizations and ministries may actually work at cross-purposes with goals to develop people. Transition from betterment to development is necessary. Yet change is never easy. How do we navigate this shift with minimal disruption and maintain the goodwill of dedicated volunteers and staff still vested in existing programs?

A short while ago, a group of concerned church and ministry leaders came to me, saying, "We would like to transition out of our giveaway programs." They witnessed the never-ending

lines of nameless recipients, many of the same ones returning month after month, year after year, coming for handouts
of food, clothes, and benevolence dollars. They experienced
that uneasy feeling that something was not quite right. Too
impersonal, few authentic relationships, no accountability. Yet
ongoing guilt kept the system operating: the guilt of spending
nearly all their tithes and offerings on themselves, the guilt of
having so much when the recipients had so little. And so the
system continued.

The leaders recalled the hornet's nest they stirred up the
last time they considered shutting down some of these programs. To the women who were the driving force behind
clothing collections and food drives, investing countless hours
in recruiting, promoting, sorting, stocking, distributing—the
very hint of terminating any of these ministries was anathema.
It would be like turning Jesus away! The subject was quickly
dropped.

"So how do we turn this corner?" the leaders asked. They
could not terminate programs in which devout members had
invested years of effort. Nor would it be productive to build a
case convincing the congregation that their traditional charity
was unhealthy and harmful. Too controversial, divisive.

I suggested beginning with an honest evaluation of each
service's benefits and limitations. It could help them decipher
the difference between "lifestyle" poverty and true emergency
needs. It would also move the discussion away from personal
investments, allowing them to take a clearer look at the goals

of their mission. Is giving to support "lifestyle" poverty really helping recipients, or is it enabling them to remain in their present condition? Questions like these help to move in the direction of change:

- Is there a way we can bring more human dignity to the process of exchange rather than simply using one-way giving?

- Can we increase our personal involvement with those in crisis to assist them with housing, day care, or other support while they get back on their feet?

At some point in the evaluation process, emotion and reason are likely to find each other. We can't save the whole world. No ministry can effectively serve across the entire spectrum of human need. To *effectively* impact a life, a relationship must be forged, trust built, accountability established. And this does not happen in long, impersonal lines of strangers.

A name and a story have to be joined to each individual face. Highly personal life struggles must be explored, and with each person a unique action plan created. A bed for the night . . . where to get a job . . . treatment for an addiction . . . escape from an abusive husband . . . childcare for homeless children . . . a wheelchair for an amputee . . . It doesn't take long to realize that the scope and depth of human need is so vast that in order to be *effective*, a group must focus in more specialized areas of service. Like affordable housing or job placement.

It is a distinctive advantage when a church is located in or near an area of need. It can become a vital center of health for the entire community. If its pastor and members live nearby, the church's power to effect change increases exponentially. Building a sense of community—so important for empowerment—is far easier when participants live in proximity rather than commute from distant, scattered locations. Daily interaction among neighbors allows relationships to develop, reciprocity to occur, and accountability to grow.

Regardless of location, however, here are a few suggestions for taking the first course-changing steps:

1. Begin with a discussion on how to support and strengthen the church's ministry to the poor.

2. Engage in an evaluation process to identify the greatest strengths and weaknesses of the current programs.

3. Research ways other ministries have increased their effectiveness (read some books and articles on the subject, making sure to include "development" material).

4. Strategize ways to become more personally, relationally involved in the lives of those you serve (begin to focus on those you are most deeply committed to).

5. Explore new options, new paradigms of service, to expand current ministries in a more holistic direction (without devaluing current ministries).

6. Identify new leadership to go on point for new initiatives

(adding new energy to the existing ministry team without threatening the dedicated volunteers who have labored long to maintain the mercy approach).

7. Once buy-in for the new paradigm has been secured, the door has opened to move ahead with change.

Change, any change, can be a painfully slow process within an established church. For entrepreneurial types, this may be an agonizing process. That's why very often creative initiatives such as this take place outside the structures of the church—which is not a bad idea. Regardless of what approach seems most workable (within or outside church bureaucracy), mercy ministries and development ministries need each other—clearly a "both/and" rather than an "either/or" matter.

## *What a Good Service Project Looks Like*

WHEN A CHURCH HAS made a commitment to partner with a community to move past betterment, beyond handouts, and toward sustainable development, volunteer involvement takes on increased meaning.

Service needs to have meaning. Simply picking up trash or hacking back overgrowth is not a meaningful task unless it is a needed part of a larger vision to impact a community. Who would give money and commit Saturdays of labor to build a Habitat house if they knew that it would soon be inhabited by drug dealers? No, we must know that a worthy poor family will permanently benefit from our efforts. Our work has to count for something of lasting value.

A World War II concentration-camp prisoner recounts the experience of Jews ordered to haul piles of rock from one end of their compound to the other, and then move them back the following day. Day after day they were ordered to do this and with disastrous results. Labor without meaning depleted their spirits. The men sickened and died in astounding numbers. Aimless toil is a curse on the human spirit.

The responsibility for a meaningful day or week (or more) of service lies jointly with both the serving and receiving groups. Volunteers have a right to expect that their efforts will make a real difference.

Planning and executing a good service experience requires a substantial amount of preparation. Talk to anyone who has coordinated a Habitat project for a church, and you will quickly realize that there is far more to building a house than raising the money and recruiting ten Saturdays of volunteers. The list of the church responsibilities is long: identifying skills, assigning team leaders, scheduling tasks, having proper tools, lining up food, distributing maps, arranging transportation . . . the list goes on. Competent management is key. Someone in the church skilled in this area has to assume the leadership role if the project is to be a satisfying one. That's the church side of the equation.

At the grass-roots level a parallel but much longer list is required to build a house. The nonprofit partner has a different, equally essential set of tasks to accomplish. Preparing the future homeowner, securing a buildable lot, selecting house plans, getting building permits, lining up appropriate subcontractors, ordering materials, providing on-site supervision . . . this list is substantially more complicated than the church's list. And the challenge of such a joint effort between church and urban ministry is far more complex than a routine construction job. Two cultures are merging, differing values and expectations are intertwining, distinctive agendas are converging around a similar vision. If done well, the relationship can be complementary and rewarding. But it will take candid conversations about expectations and ample planning and preparation.

The best service projects are joint ventures where the need is real and the vision compelling, the work is organized and productive, and the interests of both groups are satisfied. Here are a few suggestions that can help make this happen:

- Planning meeting. The leader (or leadership team) of the church meets with the leadership of the urban ministry well in advance of the proposed service project to candidly discuss expectations (what does each want to get out of this), roles (who does what), money (who is responsible for which resources), and timing (when the project will take place).

- Reaching agreement. Written communication is drafted that outlines the specific expectations, roles, and responsibilities that have been mutually agreed upon. Written memos help keep communication clear.

- Schedule. The date(s) of the project is agreed upon, and a communication schedule is established to check in with each other to see how each is proceeding on planned responsibilities. Seldom does a project turn out exactly the way it was originally conceived; thus midcourse corrections become necessary.

- Last-minute check-in. The leaders from both participating partner groups meet in person to go over the minutia of the project to assure each other that all the bases are covered. Depending upon the complexity of the project, ample lead time is allowed to do an on-site walk-through, fill any gaps, and adapt to any changes that may have developed.

- Launch. At the specific time agreed upon, volunteers, supervisors, tools, and materials converge on the site, the mission is described, assignments are given, and the work begins. There is little that makes a volunteer feel more valued than a timely, well-managed, well-executed plan—all driven by a redemptive purpose.

- Fellowship. While working alongside one another is enjoyable, planned breaks, lunches (food!), and discussion enhances the experience, especially if someone from the community joins the group to tell stories that add color and human interest to the mission.

- Meaning. Again, help volunteers understand the significance of the work. A "here's what we have accomplished" speech from the urban-ministry leader (or minister) places the work in the larger context so volunteers can appreciate its significance. Personal accounts of a project's meaning and a ceremony of dedication, etc. can add significance to the effort.

One of the most experienced organizations in running successful service projects is World Vision. One of the largest and most holistic faith-based aid and development organizations, it has a history of executing well-run service opportunities. World Vision's training materials are excellent and available online to groups interested in serving the poor, both domestically and internationally. They offer a broad range of volunteer programs, which they direct, and also welcome other groups to utilize their videos and study materials. These can be accessed through their website: www.worldvision.org.

CHARITY ORIGINATES IN THE heart. It flows out to touch a hurting world. Compassion is the reflection of the divine, the in-person reassurance that there is care in our universe. But as we have seen, charity can be either toxic or transformative. To be ultimately redemptive, it must be carefully considered. Rushing in to rescue victims from calamity may be the very highest and noblest of acts. Partnering and investing with those entrapped in chronic need is an equally noble response.

Wisdom is required to determine which is the more appropriate course in each particular case.

In this book I have attempted to map a course: from heart responses to mindful involvement with those in need—a progression from spontaneous acts of compassion to thoughtful paths to development. And I have also tried to underscore the importance of transforming the environments—the villages and neighborhoods—where the poor are often isolated.

Toxicity in the compassion industry is epidemic. This book has taken off the gloves and hit it straight on. But there is little satisfaction in criticizing the very actions that embody so much hope for a hurting world. The only gratification in writing this book lies in the possibility that a corrective shift will take place—a reversal of hurtful practices and a replacement with works that are truly good.

It is exciting to imagine the dramatic changes that would take place in this world if the enormous reserves of compassionate energy were channeled into wise, well-conceived efforts. Think of the transformation that would occur if mission trips were converted from make-work to development work; if soup kitchen servanthood were redirected to afford homeless men the dignity of securing their own food; if Saturday service projects shifted from pity to partnership; if government giveaways became accountable investments. Charity would become empowering. Victimhood would become a temporary status. Development would become the norm.

Actually, this does not call for drastic change. All it requires is for caring people to ask an honest question before they engage in service: is the need crisis or chronic? Then simply insist upon the appropriate course of action. Our hearts will continue to respond to the plight of those in dire emergencies, but our care will become more discerning as the immediate crisis passes and the time for rebuilding arrives. We will begin to require this level of candor and responsibility from those who would direct our aid.

Perhaps the most intractable aspect of such a change is mind-set. Service seeks a need, a problem to fix, an object to pity. But pity diminishes and respect emerges when servers find surprising strengths among the served, strengths not initially apparent when the served are seen as the nameless, needy poor. Perceptions change when servers discover unseen capacities, like the amazing ingenuity required to survive in harsh environments, or the deep faith that depends upon God for daily bread, or the sense of community that sacrificially shares meager resources so that those most vulnerable can survive. Authentic relationships with those in need have a way of correcting the we-will-rescue-you mind-set and replacing it with mutual admiration and respect—like the change that took place in the relationships between the suburban church volunteers who prepared Wednesday noon meals for the poor in our community and the ladies who were originally the objects of their charity. As "the poor" in the food line became people with names and familiar faces, as personal stories were exchanged, friendships began to develop. The served were eventually invited to help serve food and even assist with food preparation. Mutuality grew. New recipe ideas were explored. Culinary skills were exchanged. While sweating together in the kitchen, the lifelong dream of four of the "recipient" women eventually surfaced—to have their own restaurant.

Such a dream would be idle fantasy if not connected to resources. But these four urban women now had connected friends who did have resources. Wednesday lunches became visioning sessions for the creation of a community restaurant. Professional expertise was recruited to help outline a plan. A wider circle of friends was drawn into the vision. Money was raised. A location was secured. The excitement culminated in the grand opening of Tummy & Soul—one of the best down-home eateries on the south side.

The servers are now being served by those they once pitied.

If there is one take-away message that this book can offer to those in service work or supporting it, it is this: the poor, no matter how destitute, have enormous untapped capacity; find it, be inspired by it, and build upon it.

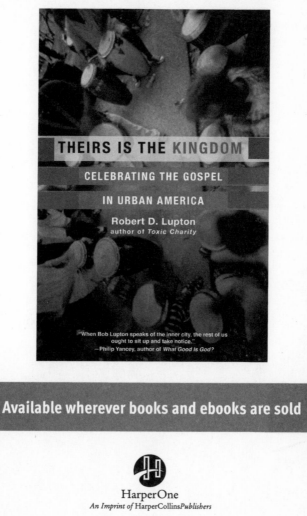